## ASSESSMENT AND LEARNING:
# THE ICE APPROACH

# ASSESSMENT AND LEARNING:
# THE ICE APPROACH

SUE FOSTATY YOUNG • ROBERT J. WILSON

PORTAGE & MAIN PRESS
(PEGUIS PUBLISHERS)

Winnipeg • Canada

Printed and bound in Canada by Printcrafters Inc.

04  5  4  3  2

Portage & Main Press acknowledges the financial support of the Government of Canada through the Book Publishing Industry Development Program (BPIDP) for our publishing activities.

**Canadian Cataloguing in Publication Data**

Fostaty Young, C. Susan,  1957–

    Assessment and learning  :  the ICE approach

    Includes bibliographical references.
    ISBN 1-894110-64-1

1. Learning    I. Wilson, Robert J.    II. Title.

LB1060.F67 2000   370.15'23   C00-920178-5

© *The Poetry of Robert Frost.* Edited by Edward Connery Lathem. New York: Henry Holt & Co. Publishers, 1969.

Book and Cover Design: Suzanne Gallant

 **PORTAGE & MAIN PRESS**
**(PEGUIS PUBLISHERS)**

100-318 McDermot Avenue
Winnipeg, Manitoba, Canada R3A 0A2
Email: books@peguis.com
Tel.: 204-987-3500
Toll free: 800-667-9673
Fax: 204-947-0080

# Contents

## Acknowledgments

Perhaps no educational practice reveals as much about a teacher's philosophies, beliefs, and values about teaching and learning as well as assessment does. Assessment is a public declaration of what is valued.

Sincere thanks go to the teachers who shared their trials and successes in the evolution of their assessment practices to ones that accurately represent what they hold to be true about teaching and learning. Thanks, too, to the students in their classes who willingly offered their own insights into the effects of the process.

# CHAPTER 1

# Ideas, Connections, and Extensions

## Introduction to ICE

Most assessment of student work in schools is a combination of normative and criterion assessment. Normative assessment makes comparisons among students; criterion assessment makes comparisons to standards and outcomes. Report cards illustrate these tendencies when they award letter grades (largely normative) along with comments (largely criterion). Teachers adopt these models because of reporting requirements and tradition.

Both normative and criterion referenced assessment are product based. How well does the student's finished work match up with expected outcomes (criteria) or with the work of others (normative)? These assessments are useful for one of the teacher's most important tasks—reporting to others. They are not very useful, however, in providing ongoing information about the processes students are using to learn.

These processes, we have found through research, tend to follow a similar pattern no matter who is doing the learning or what he or she is learning about. Consider the first time you ever sat down at a computer. First, you needed to know how to turn the machine on (and even more important, how to turn it off!). Most of us then needed a set routine, a tutorial that we carefully followed to discover how to word-process or send and receive e-mail. It was only after these basic steps were mastered, made into a routine, that we began to see how shortcuts could be taken. Instead of going back and correcting a misspelled word, we could just click on the word, look at the suggested spellings that were given, and select the right one. No need to retype. When we have mastered a routine, we seldom have to go through all the steps in a rigid manner. We take shortcuts.

Going beyond these shortcuts, learners sometimes begin to work creatively with their learning, turning it into something else entirely. For example, students copy letters, in printing or in cursive, and then they join them into words. Some students take this learning and develop their artistic expression, often spinning out elaborate ways to represent their names or signatures. This "moving beyond" the learning into new and creative areas characterizes learning that is truly one's own.

Much of teaching is about helping learners grow in their learning. Information that would be useful to teachers is that which tells where learners are in their growth. The comparisons that are most useful for this kind of assessment would not be to standards or to norms, but to the learner's own previous state. That comparison is at the heart of the ICE model and of this book.

The ICE approach is useful in that students' progress is compared to where they started from, regardless of whether that starting point is far ahead, far behind, or on par with others in the same class. Teachers are then able to give individual students the advice and tasks they need to extend learning, no matter where along the continuum they are.

Students just beginning along the growth continuum might not become as frustrated as they frequently do, because they would see evidence that they are making progress. The fact that their progress might not be as fast as someone else's becomes less significant. As for teachers, they can tailor what they want their students to know to the individual needs and characteristics of each.

The ICE approach to assessment, and the resulting recommendations for learning, occur "on the run" in classrooms. Often, it cannot be planned for in a formal way. What teachers and students need to carry out the approach is a portable tool for assessing learning growth that is easy to recall and use in both formal and informal instances. Here is where portable ICE comes into play: it is a technique for assessing growth that is portable and generalizable—across students, across subjects, across ages, and across levels of schooling.

Portable ICE is based on the premise that teachers would appreciate and use a method of assessment that could be done informally, on-the-run, and that could also assess learning growth. Some work in fields as diverse as psychology, education, and nursing has led to an understanding of how learners grow from a state of beginning to that of competence and expertise. ICE simplifies and crystallizes these stages.

The first step in the process is *Ideas*. Ideas are the building blocks of learning: the steps in a process, the necessary vocabulary, and introductory skills—all are fundamentals of the new learning. One teacher who uses ICE in his high-school classroom describes Ideas as the information that students collect from the board and their textbooks. They are the facts that are contained in their notes. He argues that when they have those fundamentals, it is "only information" —just something they possess.

Whenever we, as learners, approach something for the first time we like to know what the steps are. Until we get the hang of it, we tend to follow these steps slavishly. Think of the first time you used a computer. You had to be told where the power switch was—and then further specific details about the mouse, left clicks, icons, and the rest.

Any routine that we follow depends on Ideas. Sometimes these Ideas connect to each other in a dependent way. You have to do A before you can do B. Sometimes the steps are arbitrary. Patricia Benner, a teacher of nursing, watched novice nurses learn how to do routine nursing tasks such as taking temperatures, blood, and case histories. At first, her student nurses meticulously followed the guidelines laid out for them in their manuals. She also noticed that more experienced nurses seldom followed rules completely and thoroughly, but had learned some shortcuts that made the whole process just as effective, but more efficient.

Teachers have reported the same thing with lesson planning. While novice teachers painstakingly record each item in the lessons they prepare (these are the outcomes, these are the steps, these are the resources I will use, these are the key questions, these are the activities, and so on), experienced teachers seem to have developed strategies so that only the barest of phrases captures the steps that will follow.

Such shortcuts occur because these teachers have made *Connections* among the elements of the process, gained through repetitive use of the steps. They learn things such as: When the lesson is about this topic, we can skip steps three to five, and go immediately to step six. The situation and its characteristics are used to decide what needs to be done next. These **C**onnections occur when learners (in this case, the teachers) are able to establish and articulate relationships among the individual elements of the fundamentals. That is to say, they can tell how the **I**deas are connected.

What we want in our learners is the same kind of growth in expertise. Think of the times we ask students to tell us isolated bits of knowledge. Most completion items and multiple-choice items require this level of understanding. Such questions, if overused, actually stifle the very attribute we wish to reinforce—**C**onnections across the bits we are learning.

There is also another, deeper sense in the way that **C**onnections are made. These are the connections we make to our previous knowledge. This previous knowledge may or may not be "on the topic," but we, as humans, seem to have a need to associate new bits with things we already know. "Oh, that's just like..." we hear ourselves saying. This type of **C**onnection seems also to be related to deeper learning, learning that can be accessed and used later on.

Mathematics is a school subject that often seems to be taught without requiring the second, or deeper, level of **C**onnections to be made. Students often seem to memorize algorithms for doing routine tasks and then, if lucky, will actually be afforded the opportunity to apply these rules to problems that have been specially chosen because they fit with the rules. Problem solving is often an issue with this type of learning, because the manner in which the subject is presented and learned limits the application. A lifetime of buying tickets to movies or CDs in a music store may not be enough to see that differences in prices follow a mathematical formula—in this case the formula for the straight line. To enhance a deep understanding of any topic or subject, one must encourage students to make Connections from what they already know to what they are now learning.

*Extensions* are the final stage in growth of learning and occur when individuals no longer need to refer to the rules for operations and no longer make conscious connections among the bits or even to their own experience. At this stage, learners seem to internalize the learning to such a degree that it helps to define them as people. This internalization enables learners to answer the extrapolative question: "So, what does this mean to the way I now view the world?" New learning is created in unique and creative ways from old learning and may possibly be quite removed from the original context of the learning situation and environment. Rules will have been abandoned for "maxims," portable truths that have meaning even if they are seldom expressed and may not even be capable of expression.

Each phase of learning, Ideas, Connections, and Extensions, represents a stage of learning development—movement from novice toward expert, from superficial to deep.

**IDEAS** are demonstrated when students convey:
- the fundamentals
- basic facts
- vocabulary/definitions
- details
- elemental concepts

**CONNECTIONS** are made when students:
- demonstrate the relationship or connection among the basic concepts
- demonstrate a relationship or connection between what was learned and what they already know

**EXTENSIONS** are revealed when students:
- use their new learning in novel ways, apart from the initial learning situation
- answer the hypothetical questions: So, what does this mean? How does this shape my view of the world?

## The Theory Behind ICE

Bloom's Taxonomy, one of the earliest attempts in the 1950s to describe developments in achievement, originated out of a behaviorist notion of learning. In fact, behavior was equated with learning. In the decades that followed, psychologists of learning began to appreciate that learning was more than just an acquired response to stimuli, and that internal events were occurring that shaped the responses people made to events.

Taxonomies like Bloom's also emphasized the products of learning. In the behaviorist model, it was not important what the learner was doing during the process, only what the outcomes looked like.

In the almost half century since the publication of this and like taxonomies, cognitive psychologists have come a long way in understanding the mechanisms people use to move from little knowledge to a lot. Some learners, for example, habitually use "surface" approaches to learning, content with attempting to match their learning to the specific demands of the task. Often, schools unintentionally support such learning approaches by a too-heavy reliance on multiple-choice and completion-type assessments.

A more effective approach, both to teaching and assessment, emphasizes depth of learning more than coverage. Different strategies are required when the purpose becomes one of helping learners see connections among the bits and pieces of learning and relate all of it to previous understandings. In a "one size fits all" assessment scheme, for example, it is difficult to honor these individual patterns. So is a teaching approach that demands all students learn the same things and to the same level of understanding. (For those wishing to explore these matters in more detail, an annotated bibliography is provided at the end of this book.)

Once it was possible to think of learning in this way, it also became possible to think of growth in learning. No longer was it merely a bit by bit accumulation of discrete information, but it was manipulated, altered, and transformed inside the head of the learner.

The dominance in some schools of assessment tools that still reflect the behaviorist idea—lots of short answer, fill in the blanks, and multiple choice—means that these developments have not been universally adopted. Even fairly recent developments in the use of rubrics still cling to a notion that more is equivalent to better.

Two of the earlier proponents of cognitive change in students' achievement were John Biggs and Kevin Collis (1982). They examined the way students, at several ages, responded to a variety of questions in a variety of subjects. They developed a new taxonomy that they called SOLO (Structure of Observed Learning Outcomes). Patricia Benner (1984) was similarly struck by how her novice nurses developed in the skills needed to become proficient in the nursing field.

Following a Piagetian view of cognitive development (without being too committed to stage theory), Biggs and Collis analyzed student responses. Based on those responses, they devised five categories:

1. Prestructural Level: In this stage, the lowest category, the learner has little idea about how to even approach the question and, as a result, produces irrelevant or non-responses to the question posed.

2. Unistructural Level: At this stage, the learner selects one single piece of information and focuses on that to the exclusion of anything else.

3. Multistructural Level: Learners produce more than one piece of information, but in the form of a list with no attempt to link one piece to another.

4. Relational Level: At this later stage, learners tie together the pieces of information under headings or categories.

5. Extended Abstract Level: Finally, learners take the learning and carry it further, into a new mode of discourse.

Another interesting aspect of Biggs and Collis's work was that they developed their theory from looking at the responses real learners made to real questions in a variety of subjects.

Benner, in her work, watched prospective nurses carry out procedures. For example, when a nurse was administering a drug or taking a blood sample, she would follow the procedures rigidly at first until she gained experience. Later, the nurse would see the relationships among the steps and realize that she could combine steps or even omit them in certain situations without jeopardizing the patient's well being. When the nurse became expert, she noticed characteristics of the patient (a collection of fluid in the arm) that stopped her from taking blood entirely and allowed her to pursue a new line of inquiry.

Notice that the same principles of learning development occur whether one is dealing with a physical skill or a mental operation. In the behaviorist tradition, learning was compartmentalized artificially into domains of knowledge (cognitive, affective, psychomotor) as though these were discrete, unconnected processes. We now know that learning in every domain is influenced by cognitive activity. Thus, it would be possible that a learner in one situation may exhibit a quite different level of functioning than she/he would in another situation— a characteristic we see all the time in learners.

Neither Biggs and Collis nor Benner saw their new taxonomies as portable. What we have done in this book is simplified the "novice to expert" literature to provide a view of growth that teachers can carry around with them and access at all times. Not only can teachers carry it around, but learners can too, so that they can be monitors of their own development. We hope we have not lost the essence of their understanding in the simplification and summarizing we have done.

# CHAPTER 2

# Applying ICE to Teaching and Learning

The whole notion of ICE began as a model to describe the developmental nature of learning so that teachers might better understand how to foster that development in their classrooms. The premise is that through improved understanding and appreciation of the learning process, we, as teachers, might be better able to facilitate it.

The two, teaching and learning, are necessarily inseparable. Decisions that teachers make about how and what to teach are based on who their students are, what those students know, how the students learn, and what the purpose of the learning is. The process of teaching and learning begins, continues, and draws to a close through a continuum of learning assessment and teaching response that occurs through monitoring learners' progress.

Teachers make judgments about the nature of students' learning on an ongoing basis that help to inform their decisions about how and what to teach next. Using both formal and informal methods, they develop a sixth sense when it comes to learning assessment, becoming able to quickly determine the quality of individual student's understanding. Despite the development of this sixth sense, teachers may have difficulty pin-pointing the specific characteristics, or markers, that help them differentiate between progressive levels of students' learning.

The framework provided in ICE helps to clarify the characteristics and markers that indicate where learners are along the learning continuum and, in so doing, enables teachers to make instructional decisions that maximize learning. The following example of ICE in action may help to illustrate the framework and its potential benefits to learning and teaching.

*    *    *

Jeanette Bouvier's grade-eight students were asked to write a short essay about the personal meaning they found in Robert Frost's poem *Mending Wall.* As expected, the range of responses to the task was varied, yet Jeanette had little difficulty deciding which of the essays merited high grades and which ones fell short of her expectations for a final draft. To her trained eye, some *were just better,* and any teacher would be likely to rank them the same way. She is probably right, but using ICE enabled her to make judgments that were based on more than just instinct about what good answers look like. Moreover, the framework helped her formulate responses to the essays that encouraged continued growth for each student, no matter how thorough or limited their initial answers to the question were.

Mending Wall

Something there is that doesn't love a wall,
That sends the frozen-ground-swell under it,
And spills the upper boulders in the sun;
And makes gaps even two can pass abreast.
The work of hunters is another thing:
I have come after them and made repair
Where they have left not one stone on a stone,
But they would have the rabbit out of hiding,
To please the yelping dogs. The gaps I mean,
No one has seen them made or heard them made,
But at spring mending-time we find them there.
I let my neighbour know beyond the hill;
And on a day we meet to walk the line
And set the wall between us once again.
We keep the wall between us as we go.
To each the boulders that have fallen to each.
And some are loaves and some so nearly balls
We have to use a spell to make them balance:
"Stay where you are until our backs are turned!"
We wear our fingers rough with handling them.
Oh, just another kind of outdoor game,
One on a side. It comes to little more:
There where it is we do not need the wall:
He is all pine and I am apple orchard.
My apple trees will never get across

And eat the cones under his pines, I tell him.
He only says, "Good fences make good neighbours."
Spring is the mischief in me, and I wonder
If I could put a notion in his head:
'Why do they make good neighbours? Isn't it
Where there are cows? But here there are no cows.
Before I built a wall I'd ask to know
What I was walling in or walling out,
And to whom I was like to give offence.
Something there is that doesn't love a wall,
That wants it down.' I could say 'Elves' to him,
But it's not elves exactly, and I'd rather
He said it for himself. I see him there
Bringing a stone grasped firmly by the top
In each hand, like an old-stone savage armed.
He moves in darkness as it seems to me,
Not of woods only and the shade of trees.
He will not go behind his father's saying,
And he likes having thought of it so well
He says again, "Good fences make good neighbours."

---

### My Essay about *Mending Wall*

This man lives in Maine and each Spring he has to get his neighbour out to help repair the wall that has fallend [sic] down during the winter. They walk along picking up the stones and the man wonders why they do it because he has pine trees on one side and apple trees on the other and there isn't any use in a wall being there. His neighbour does this every year because his father did it so he thinks that's good enough reason for it.

**Figure 2.1.**

In the example shown in fig. 2.1, Jeanette saw that the student had clearly gleaned the basic Ideas in the surface structure of the poem. That is, she appears to have understood the language to convey the narrative. Despite that, there is no indication that the student was able to make personal sense of the work, nor has she made an attempt to delve beyond the surface meaning. In an attempt to nudge this student beyond merely reiterating the Ideas, Jeanette might choose to invite her to offer her own opinions about the tradition of mending the fence, or ask her to draw parallels between the events of the story and an occurrence in her day-to-day life.

On Reading the Poem, *Mending Wall*, by Robert Frost

The narrator says at one point that "I'd rather he said it for himself" and that is the way he writes his poem too. He doesn't want to tell the reader what to think; he wants to show us instead. What he wants to show us is the silliness of repairing a fence where there is no need to have one. Fences are barriers and there is something unnatural about them. "We keep the wall between us as we go" means that there is no chance the narrator and the neighbour will be able to communicate with each other. The reason for that is that the narrator wants to think about things while the neighbour only wants to do what his father said was right. There are lots of things we do in life that are routine and that we do without thinking. At school for example, we do things at the bell, or we read notices before lunch and we all have to listen to them even if we don't care about volleyball or lunch clean up. This is a good poem to study in school because it explains why knowledge is so important as a way of helping us go farther than previous generations and not just accepting what has gone before without questioning it.

**Figure 2.2.**

The writer of the example in fig. 2.2 has not only indicated that he understood the surface Ideas presented in the poem, but has Connected those basic Ideas to personal life experiences to explain the meaning of the poem as represented in his own life. Moreover, he has Extended those Connections to a novel situation that helps him see the world in a new way through metaphor. Jeanette's response to this student is likely to be an invitation to read more Robert Frost or perhaps to compose an original poem on a related theme.

Jeanette was immediately intrigued by the last sentence of a third student's answer (fig. 2.3): "Another thing I liked about the poem was the mystery of why the stones fall down in the first place." She interpreted it as an indication that this student was on the verge of a learning transformation from Ideas to Connections. The comments Jeanette makes to this student might include an invitation to elaborate and offer her own interpretation of why the stones fall down—an invitation to move toward the next stage of learning growth.

**Thoughts about *Mending Wall*, by Robert Frost**

Every year the author and his neighbour meet at the wall that separates their property to fix it. The wall loses some of its stones during the winter so the wall has to be fixed in the spring. The author sees the wall as a barrier where there is no need to be one and the neighbour sees it as a custom that they have always done. So the two men meet and each walks on his side of the fence, picking up stones, and putting them back up on the wall where they will only fall down again next year. The author was trying to get us to consider the reasons behind what we do and see if they are necessary or only a tradition. He also feels that the neighbour is wrong when he says that he lives in darkness and looks like a savage carrying the stones. Another thing I liked about the poem was the mystery of why the stones fall down in the first place.

**Figure 2.3.**

In each example, the answers that the students provided were right. Jeanette judged each student's learning, not by the number of correct paraphrases and references, but by what each student did with the basic **I**deas.

## Monitoring Progress in Hard-to-Assess Areas

Virtually all classroom activities provide teachers with information that can be used to monitor learning progress. Aside from the formal and traditional unit tests, assignments, and projects, teachers gain insight into learning development in myriad informal and unstructured ways. The questions class members ask, the answers they provide, the manner in which class members interact, and individual contributions to class discussion and group work, all provide teachers with a steady stream of information that is used to monitor individual student's progress. What is more, those same data inform teachers' judgments about curriculum-content areas and decisions about the approaches to teaching that are most likely to nudge learning along from one level of competence to the next.

The processes of collecting data to inform decision-making vary widely in their form and structure. Test results and graded work provide teachers with hard numbers that are used to gauge relative success; rating scales and checklists are designed to provide at-a-glance records of behavioral demonstrations of skill development; and class participation and discussions afford teachers the opportunity to get a sense of how well students are doing in a less structured and informal environment.

The judgments made about learning during comparatively unstructured activities are based on more than just teachers' experience and good sense, although many teachers might be hard pressed to explain *how* they are able to make the judgments they do.

Norm, a graphic design teacher, reports that the progress seminars he holds prior to students' presentations of their final products are usually good predictors of students' final grades. He reports that better students tend to be very engaged in the process and notice more details about others' projects and comment on a wide variety of components. They have developed "a designer's eye." The weaker students tend to be reserved during the seminars and when invited to contribute, often say that they agree with what everyone else has already said.

While Norm can predict from the progress seminar who will finish the course with good grades, he might not be able to articulate the qualitative differences in the demonstrations of the students' learning through the seminar discussion. Using ICE as a guide would provide a framework upon which to base his judgments made during these everyday observations. What fundamentals (**I**deas) are the students competently demonstrating? What **C**onnections are they making (or missing)? How have they been able to use this learning in a novel way (**E**xtensions), and how has it shaped the way they are approaching this project? In these ways, the framework provides a basis for decision-making and gives structure, meaning, and form to all those seemingly subjective "gut feelings" that all teachers have about learners' readiness levels and competence.

## Class Discussions

Just as judgments about the quality of learning can be made through tests and assignments, there are valuable opportunities for learning assessment in the relative informality of class discussions.

*      *      *

A teacher just finished reading the story *The Boy Who Cried Wolf* to her grade-two class. She began a class discussion as a means of gauging students' comprehension. She asked the class what the story was about and what it meant. Here are some of the responses:

> *It's about a boy watching sheep. It means the town people got mad when they found out he lied.*

> *It means when you're bored you shouldn't lie to get attention.*

> *It's about what happens when you don't tell the truth. It means that when you tell lies to your friends then they won't know when to believe you.*

The responses range from one that indicates a basic understanding of the fundamentals of the story—the location, characters, and main Idea, right through to another that indicates the listener has made a Connection between the story and her real world. All three responses can be said to be right and true. The difference among them is that they each demonstrate a different level of learning development.

Being aware of the qualitative differences among those responses, and the implications of those differences, helps teachers make appropriate responses that facilitate students' movement from one level of learning toward the next. In this case, the teacher may choose to pose additional questions designed to nudge each student toward awareness of the next stage of learning.

In many cases, teachers set the tone for class discussions by the quality of their focus questions. That is not to say that questions in and of themselves are inherently good or bad. It means that each question posed for discussion may, by its nature and quality, cue responses of predetermined quality.

Some questions are posed that tend to encourage responses that are restricted to the reiteration of Ideas. They are typically closed questions that require factual responses to demonstrate comprehension or retention. In discussing an assigned novel, a teacher may ascertain who has read the book by asking reiterative questions such as:

> Who are the characters in the story?
> What happened first?
> Where does the story take place?

The nature of other questions ICE might elicit responses that require learners to make Connections; learners are invited to establish relationships between the presented ideas or to build relationships and Connections between the material and their own experiences:

> How does the author establish the tone of the book?
> How realistic is this novel?
> What impact does (event A) have on the main character?

While the wording of the questions can be easily modified to suit the age and grade levels of the students participating in the discussion, the intent will remain constant. For students who are not yet able to make Connections, teachers might choose to make use of bridging, or leading questions, to facilitate the transition. Such questions might include:

> How did you feel when you read the book?
> What words and scenes did the author use that helped make you feel that way?

In this way, the teacher begins at the Ideas level and invites the student to attempt a well-defined Connection.

Still, other forms of questions may help to nudge participants to make Extensions—to extrapolate their learning to novel situations with an implicit invitation to answer questions about how the new learning affects their evolving view of the world. For example, you may ask the following questions:

> Explain how the story might have been different if the main character had been a girl.

How has the story influenced the way you think about...?

While the form of these questions is open-ended enough to invite Extensions, the questions are still accessible to all students to answer at any stage of learning development.

In order to maximize the benefit of class discussions, it is imperative that teachers articulate what the specific objectives or learning outcomes of the discussion are to be. Once that has been established, discussion questions should invite participation at every level of learning development. That is not to say that teachers should attempt to elicit predetermined responses to their questions, but rather, they should attempt to provide opportunities for all students to demonstrate attainment of those outcomes at varying levels of learning development. Discussion questions, then, should be as purposeful and well thought out as those for examination purposes.

Sample Question Starters

How many times have teachers heard students complain that the questions on a test did not give them an opportunity to show how much they knew? That complaint may arise when students are capable of demonstrating learning beyond Ideas-level learning, but are not invited to do so as part of the assessment process. Teachers can guard against restricting their students by designing questions that can be answered at a number of different levels.

Questions can be purposefully designed to elicit, and limit, responses to specific and predetermined levels of learning. That is, teachers can issue invitations to students to demonstrate specific levels of learning through careful wording of their questions. Consider the examples of question starters in fig. 2.4 and the range in quality of the responses they are likely to yield.

Notice, for example, that the invitation to *Explain the relationship between...*is constructed as an explicit invitation to make Connections. Yet, it is also flexible enough to accommodate responses from students at the Ideas level (who might just list qualities of each aspect rather than explain a relationship), or the Extensions level of learning (who may extrapolate to hypothetical situations). Good quality questions will be accessible to *all* students, at some level, yet extendable by some.

| Ideas | Connections | Extensions |
|-------|-------------|------------|
| ■ List the… | ■ What effect does _____ have on… | ■ Predict how… |
| ■ Identify the main… | ■ Estimate… | ■ Propose solutions for… |
| ■ Give examples from the text of… | ■ What alternative methods… | * ■ What are the implications of… |
| ■ Paraphrase..... | * ■ Of what value is… | * ■ In your opinion… |
| ■ Who was… | * ■ Explain the relationship between… | * ■ What did you learn from… |
| ■ When did… | * ■ How is _____ like… | |
| ■ According to…how is… | * ■ Compare… | |
| | * ■ Using an example from your own experience, illustrate… | |

**Figure 2.4.** Examples of question starters.

\* Examples of questions that are accessible to all students, yet extendable.

**Guidelines for Developing Good Discussion Questions**

1. Establish a supportive environment where questioning is valued and "thinking out loud" is not only accepted, but encouraged. To help create that support:
   - Provide thinking time between posing the questions and expecting a response.
   - Ensure that questions are open to everyone before inviting a response from any one particular student.
   - Expect and encourage diversity—few things squelch creativity and experimentation with ideas as quickly as being told you are wrong because your answer differed from the teacher's expectation.
   - Accept all responses as worthwhile demonstrations of comprehension and learning development. Use the presented opportunity to clarify, reiterate, or reteach, as necessary.

2. Know and articulate the objectives or outcomes you hope to address through the planned discussion.

3. Use open-questions rather than closed-questions so that students will not be confined to yes/no options or to one-dimensional responses.
   - The purpose of discussion questions is not to elicit basic information, but to provide some insight into students' thought processes.

4. Questions should be accessible to all students and extendable by some.
   - Formulate questions in such a way as to be open to a variety of response levels. Asking questions that are specifically designed to elicit responses at the **I**deas or **C**onnections level may limit responses to that level even if students are capable of more. Similarly, questions that have been specifically designed to evoke **E**xtensions may exclude responses from students who are able to make **C**onnections or who have a good grasp of the fundamentals (**I**deas).
   - While posing progressively higher-level questions may seem like a good idea, it is likely that fewer students will be able to participate in the discussion as questioning escalates. Posing questions that are open to a variety of response levels allows the teacher to assess the content of each response as it is offered, allowing him or her to assess each participant's contribution. The teacher may respond immediately to gauge current levels of understanding or to nudge learning toward the next level. It is also much more likely that teachers will be able to recall students' responses than they will be able to recall who stopped participating at what level of questioning.

## Group and Experiential Work

Classroom learning has evolved over time from individualistic, teacher-centered activity toward more collaborative, learner-centered endeavours. The single-person desks of the past have been complemented by, or replaced with, work stations and tables to accommodate learning groups; top-down teaching is being supplemented by more participation, discovery, experimentation, and experiential methods.

In the face of these changes, the debate among experiential educators continues over whether experiences can be assessed effectively and over how best to assess group work. In one graduate-level course, one student put forth the argument that since it was impossible for students to have only half of, or one third of, an experience, everyone in the Outdoor and Experiential Education course must be awarded an "A" as a final grade. The ensuing discussion yielded a caution to students and teachers alike: It is the *learning that results from the experience* that must be assessed, not participation in the experience itself. For this reason, it is critically important for teachers to select experiential focus-activities with care. All too often, experiential activities are selected because they are fun, engaging, and encourage high levels of learner participation. Unfortunately, they may provide little in terms of learning effectiveness if they are misused or discontinued before Connections can be made.

*     *     *

John C., teaching data management to his grade-two class, decided to change his approach. He wanted his students to consider how objects can have more than one attribute, and how this affects data collection. He also wanted his students to accomplish the task actively.

He supplied each group of four students with a box of everyday objects—a book, a stapler, gum, a spoon, string, red and blue circles and squares, a magazine, paper toweling, a bottle of glue, a prism, scissors, and other things. He instructed the class to work in groups to sort the objects into five predetermined categories that described variables of color, shape, material, and function. After 15 minutes of animated interaction, Mr. C. asked each group to disclose the items in each category. It was discovered that the sum of all the categorized objects was greater than the number of objects in each of the boxes. Mr. C. then asked his class to explain that occurrence to him.

Mr. C. knew that he would not be able to do more than nudge the grade-two class toward understanding the complex concept of multiple attributes without extending the original activity beyond its introductory stage. He asked the groups to share their results and pointed out that the stapler seemed to have been categorized at least three different ways. Questions were posed to the class that encouraged them to consider how that could possibly have happened. The groups then went back to their tables for more sorting according to their own categories.

As a whole class follow-up activity, the children tried to categorize themselves in as many ways as possible. A discussion ensued about methods of categorizing a host of classroom objects until Mr. C. was satisfied that the children understood the concept of multiple attributes. That decision was made as a result of his ongoing appraisal of the learning being demonstrated.

In addition to providing his students with a memorable, participatory experience, Mr. C. managed to maximize the learning that occurred. He planned the event and the questions deliberately enough to nudge the children toward learning, and flexibly enough that they made the discoveries and the inferences on their own—the hallmark of experiential learning.

1. Base all focus-activity selections on learning outcomes.
   - Know and be able to articulate the specific learning outcomes you are working toward before your activity search.
   - Modify the activities to meet your stated learning outcomes. Ask: *How can I manipulate this activity to teach this outcome?* If you find yourself asking: *What can I teach by using this activity?* you're going backward.

2. Design a series of questions as a follow-up to the focus exercise.
   - Questions should encourage students to reflect on the focus-experience in such a way as to invite them to create their own theories, make connections, and to extrapolate from the focus experience to the curriculum and to the real world.
   - Follow the "Guidelines for Developing Good Discussion Questions."

3. Evaluate the relative merits of the experiential exercise.
   - Teachers should review and modify classroom activities after use in much the same way as they review and modify their tests to be sound and reliable.

Guidelines for Selecting and Using Experiential Learning Activities

- If an activity yields less than stellar results, analyze the way it was introduced, used, monitored, and discussed. It may be that minor adjustments to the presentation are all that are needed to get more focused learning results.

4. If applicable, assess the process elements of the group or experiential task.

   - Group work has at least two elemental components contributing to the relative outcome of the work: product and process. The *product* outcomes are those that are comparatively easy to assess. They involve a comparison of the group's final product with a set of previously established and articulated criteria. The crux of the product-assessment question centers on how well the group produced what it had set out to.

   The *process* outcomes pertain to the relationships within the group: the maintenance of the relationships during the completion of the product and the manner in which the product was completed—the *how* as opposed to the *what*. As part of experiential focus exercises, the process also requires participants to reflect upon the implications of the event and its influences on learning and on group functioning.

   Process outcomes such as cooperation and collaborative skills are highly valued, both in the classroom and by employers, yet it is uncommon for them to be formally assessed in classroom settings. The focus of assessment is usually on the product in spite of teachers' interest in developing the process skills. ICE proves to be a useful tool in assessing and developing the process skills.

   As with product outcomes, the critical first step in assessing process outcomes is in articulating what they are. What process skills do you hope to develop? Group problem solving? Conflict resolution? Leadership management? What evidence indicates acquisition of those skills? What will demonstration of the fundamentals (**I**deas) look like compared to evidence of **C**onnections?

Once the specific learning outcomes of experiential or group exercises have been established, teachers will have an easier time articulating the ranges of responses they are likely to elicit with their follow-up questions.

## Journal Assessment

Learning journals have become a popular tool for tracking learning. Through journal entries, learners work through thought processes, document participation in field placements, or reflect upon the results of experiential focus exercises, and share learning insights. Despite the fact that teachers value the potential learning that may result from keeping a reflective learning journal, many have expressed skepticism about the feasibility of assessing journal entries as they would other products of learning.

For example, the co-op teachers we spoke with all agreed that having a journal requirement in their courses was one of their keys to a successful semester:

> *Since I can't be in 32 places at once, having them keep journals is one of the few ways I have of monitoring their co-op experiences. They keep logs of their work days and are supposed to detail problems they encounter by applying some of the concepts we cover in class to work out a potential solution.*

> *I use journals in my Early Childhood Education course. It's a great way for the students, and me, to see where the gaps in their learning are and where their strengths lie.*

> *Even some of the students have commented on what a great way it is for them to organize their thoughts about what they've learned—they get to test things out on paper and give themselves a mental stretch, write notes to themselves, whatever, before having to use the stuff in real life, or on a test.*

The conversation was animated as the teachers enthused over the positive effects of using journals as learning tools. Yet, when the question of grading those same journals arose, the tenor of the discussion changed considerably.

> *No, they're not graded. I require that they're done. It's not worth anything, grade-wise, in and of itself. It's kind of hard to do that, unless you give marks for...I don't know - spelling?*

*Oh, I grade journals like everyone else in my department. There are 15 or 20 marks in the evaluation scheme for journals. If you hand in a journal, you get the mark; if you don't, you don't.*

*The range of the stuff that gets handed in is incredible! Sometimes it bothers me that I end up giving the same grade to each journal when some of them are so detailed and others are cursory rehashes. There must be a better way than giving away 15 or 20% of the final grade, but it would be SO subjective!*

By reading journals within the ICE framework, teachers make more than subjective judgments about the quality of learning demonstrated through the medium, regardless of grade level. They determine the level of learning demonstrated through each entry and may even be able to pinpoint *where* learning growth begins to develop.

Entries that demonstrate basic understanding of the course vocabulary and fundamental concepts are indicative of **I**deas-level learning. They typically include reiterative entries based on content, class events, schedules, and notes. Then, there will be entries that seem a little more involved indicating that learners have moved beyond **I**deas. When entries link individual concepts together in such a way that demonstrates an appreciation of the relationships between them, students have begun to make **C**onnections within the learning. When entries indicate that learners have been able to answer the question: "So what does all this mean to the way I now see the world?" they have reached the **E**xtensions phase of learning development.

*       *       *

The following journal entries are samples submitted by three Continuing Education college students who participated in a Group Dynamics course. Following a brief discussion about the rationale for the journal requirement, participants were asked to make regular journal entries to demonstrate their understanding of the concepts covered in each class.

**February 12**

Today we learned about positive interdependence. Interdependence refers to how group members interact and rely on each other to achieve group goals. There is positive interdependence (collaboration) and negative interdependence (competition). Groups should work toward positive interdependence to be effective. There are many factors that influence a group's level of interdependence: group size, task, member expertise, reward structures, time constraints, interpretation of member roles, etc.

I learned a lot in today's class about why so many groups fail! Sometimes there's a mismatch between goal structures and what you want the group to end up doing, and it ends up that the group does exactly the opposite of what you had planned, but it's because it wasn't set up properly.

**Figure 2.5.**

It is clear that this student (fig. 2.5) has a firm grasp of the **I**deas that were discussed in class. There is a demonstration of knowledge of the terminology and meaning through the reiteration of the session's content. The comments at the end of the entry about mismatched goal structures and group function may indicate readiness for a movement toward **C**onnections, but are, as yet, tentative. Careful selection of focus questions on the teacher's part might help nudge this student toward further exploration in that direction. Even a simple invitation by the teacher for the student to share an example from her own experience might be all that is necessary.

Using the ideas presented in class, the following student (fig. 2.6) has been able to use his own terms to define the concepts. He has made **C**onnections between the theory presented in the class and his own group's functioning, something that has been encouraged from the outset. Additionally, he has made the **C**onnection between the course material and his own reality.

**February 12**

Our group is working well because we have positive social interdependence. We know that the contributions of each member are what makes our group tick. Arthur is great when it comes to the technical things for our presentation; Serge keeps us on track—he's our manager; we rely on Jaqueline to act as process observer; and I bring material from my Human Resources class to share with everyone (member roles). We each have a strong sense of each other's contributions and we know that each part is important to our success. After thinking about ways to increase interdependence, I had a look at the grading scheme for the course. It's been designed to help increase our reliance on each other! The grades we earn are related to how well we help each other become effective! I hadn't realized how that could affect the way groups work, until now.

**Figure 2.6.**

Notice that fig. 2.5 is interesting because it differs from fig. 2.6. in both *quality* and *quantity*. Even though the first sample includes many more individual pieces of course content (**I**deas) than the second sample, the first student has not demonstrated that any specific **C**onnections have been made between those **I**deas, nor has she demonstrated that she has been able to relate the "bits" to any of her previous learning.

The journal entry in fig. 2.7 shows that this student has been able to **E**xtend her learning from the classroom to a novel situation quite removed from the learning environment. She has **E**xtended the learned material and answers the "so what" question by indicating how her learning has had an effect on how she now views the world.

As with any other teaching/assessment tool, journals should be used to elicit specific outcomes. When those outcomes have been clearly defined and articulated, learners are able to use the journals to their best advantage. Additionally, when outcomes and rationales are articulated clearly and understood by all, then judgments made about the demonstrations of learning have base and form.

**February 12**

During tonight's class a light bulb went on! Now I understand why the groups at work aren't working! We're all expected to work together, pool all our skills and resources to get things done (positive interdependence), but the way the company gives bonuses to individual people for their innovations and good work seems to increase competition (negative interdependence) between group members. Competition isn't bad, but in this case it's getting in the way of having effective work teams. Getting the company to consider changing its policy to giving bonuses to teams rather than members could make the groups more productive by increasing positive interdependence and reducing competition within the teams. That would also probably increase productivity over the short term, and profits over the long term.

**Figure 2.7.**

Guidelines for Effective Use of Journals

1. Be specific about your expectations for the journal requirement.
   - Know and articulate the purpose of the journal and the learning that is to be demonstrated through it. Students must be made aware of the journal's purpose before they can determine what to include in their entries and what form their journal is to take. If the journal is to be used as a diary or for personal communication, and not as a learning tool, assessment will not be an issue to consider.
   - Outline your specific expectations for journal entries. What is appropriate to include?
2. If necessary, provide examples of journal entries at a variety of learning levels or at levels that are representative of your expectations.
3. Consider alternative formats for journaling.
   - If appropriate, consider offering the option of audio-taped entries, pictorial entries, or other suitable formats.

4. Offer the option of providing daily or weekly focus questions for students to reflect upon until they become familiar with the journaling process.

   ■ Focus questions will be entirely dependent on the learning you hope to elicit.

5. To maximize learning, review journals and offer constructive feedback early in the learning process.

## Projects, Presentations, and Assignments

In most instances, projects and assignments are used as means of generating grades for reporting purposes. While grading will be dealt with more thoroughly as a topic in its own right in a subsequent section, it is imperative to acknowledge the dual purposes of many assigned learning tasks.

Good assignments and projects are designed to afford learners the opportunity to demonstrate acquired skills and knowledge; they also have the potential to challenge learners toward new levels of learning. But projects can only be expected to be as good as their articulated purposes. That is, to reap the full benefits of completing an assignment or project, it is essential that students, and teachers, be aware of the work's purpose aside from the one to generate a grade for reporting purposes.

\*     \*     \*

A grade-ten geography student had just completed a project on cannabis cultivation and the resulting commerce in British Columbia. The project had been assigned as a means of assessing students' mastery of theories and assimilation of concepts covered in the course. The results were to be used to generate a mark for the course that would contribute to the calculations for the final grade. James's work included details on the effects of geographic location on growing conditions and crop-yield, import-export and employment statistics, and graphs depicting the impact of the cannabis trade on the provincial and federal economies.

James was very pleased with the final product. Considering it some of his best work, he awarded himself an "A" in the self-evaluation. The project could just as easily have earned him a "C" if the finished product was not quite what his teacher had envisioned as a quality geography project. Fortunately, the teacher had provided her students with a rationale and explicit criteria for their demonstrations of learning. By providing a basic framework for the assignment and the expectations for demonstrations of learning, the teacher helped to focus students' efforts. She provided the opportunity for them to appreciate and assess their own learning against those markers without having to make assumptions or guesses about what demonstrations would be valued.

One teacher had a recurrence of students submitting superficial work. After learning about ICE for the first time, he confided:

> *Before I heard about this (ICE), I'd ask students for "more" in an answer, or in a project, and I'm not sure that I even knew exactly what that meant. What usually happened was that I got more words, or more pages, but not more of an answer. Now I can tell students that they've presented the basic **I**deas well, but that I'd like them to make **C**onnections. Before, I was trying to encourage them but didn't have a way of defining how to make the leap. Some students had difficulty because they didn't realize that I wanted them to go further, to take that leap from **I**deas to **C**onnections or to **E**xtensions.*

1.  Rather than assign general projects, design them to address specific learning outcomes (content).
    - Select and state the selected learning outcomes to be demonstrated and content areas to be covered in the completed project, and share them with the students. It will help them to focus their efforts on demonstrating their learning through content quality.

2.  Determine the qualities (not content) that you expect in the finished product.
    - Once content areas have been selected and articulated, concentrate on what learning demonstrations might look like in an acceptable project. What qualities will separate excellent projects from good ones? No matter what subject or grade level, teachers should describe, qualitatively, what characteristics

Guidelines for Successful Use of Projects, Presentations, and Assignments differentiate adequate, basic understanding from masterful, deep learning and what the significant factors are that distinguish growth from one level to the next.

- Once you have determined the various qualities of learning, consider that each student may now be at liberty to select individualistic ways of demonstrating that learning.

3. Be flexible regarding project formats.
   - Once you have determined the outcomes that are to be addressed and the qualities of acceptable, good, and great demonstrations of them, consider that students may demonstrate those outcomes in myriad ways—written reports, experiments, narratives, inventions, plays, journals, and videos, just to name a few.

## Mapping Progress Through Rubrics

Teachers might balk at the thought of having to assess projects and assignments that are as individual as their students' learning needs and interests. Imagine—a class of twenty-six students and everyone doing a different kind of project—research essays, experiments, and photo displays! Rubrics are the answer to the inevitable questions about subjectivity and fairness of the assessment process.

Rubrics are chart-like representations that detail the essential elements of specific learning tasks and describe characteristics of the learning at progressive levels of achievement. Usually, the elements of learning are listed vertically down the left side of the page and derive from the specific learning outcomes. The descriptors of achievement run across the top, creating an easy-to-read chart.

Because they provide a blueprint for what learning looks like at various levels of achievement, rubrics can serve as a reference and guideline for teachers' instructional delivery strategies and content organization. Rubrics have the added benefit of facilitating communication about learning acquisition between individual teachers, between teachers and students, and among teachers, parents, and administrators.

## Constructing ICE Rubrics

ICE is designed to be a portable tool. The acronym is easy to remember and the model can be applied across curriculum areas and grade levels. The stages of learning development represented by the acronym are relatively uncomplicated, and discrete, and can be easily called to mind whenever the need arises. Teachers familiar with ICE carry it with them and apply it to a wide range of subjects and learning demonstrations. Teachers who are less familiar with ICE or who want to gain better insight into the teaching and learning processes in their classrooms, and those who wish to share ICE with their students, have found writing ICE rubrics to be a valuable exercise.

Remember, rubrics are nothing more than descriptions of learning at different levels of development. There are a few different ways to approach the task. First, don't lose sight of the basics of ICE. For a quick refresher, turn back to Introduction to ICE (page 1).

If you are creating a rubric for the first time, and have already had the opportunity to assess student work, it may be helpful to have at least three pieces of work that you have already assessed without the benefit of an ICE rubric in front of you. Each piece should be representative of a different level of learning from "OK" to "Wow."

Start off by describing the qualities of each piece of work that helped you decide to evaluate it the way you did. It might even help you to start off by saying to yourself, *This student got a B because...*

Beware. When describing work that is less than top-notch, there is a tendency to describe it in terms of what has NOT been demonstrated rather than in terms of the positive qualities that were included. For example, Pauline, a primary teacher, described the products of a writing task in this way:

> *I didn't give Sean full marks because he didn't include a rough draft and there were no pictures to help illustrate the action of his story.*

This description allows insight into the expectations that the teacher had for work at the upper end of the scale, but it does not give us any insight into what was included in this student's work. Now we need an articulation of the positive characteristics of Sean's work that helped the teacher make the judgments she did about his learning.

*He did use capital letters to begin each sentence and periods to end them. So his punctuation was good. He used a couple of compound sentences that helped to increase interest, and his printing was careful and neat.*

Now we have a better idea of what Sean's writing looks like, because we have been told what *has* been demonstrated rather than what is missing. Pauline's developing rubric will include the components she has just commented on and might, before refining, begin to look like the chart shown in fig. 2.8.

| Elements | Ideas | Connections | Extensions |
|---|---|---|---|
| Legibility and Visual Appeal | ■ Forms recognizable letters<br>■ Initial draft is also the final draft | ■ Letters are grouped and spaced to form words<br>■ Creates a final draft from the original | ■ Words follow in logical sequence<br>■ Includes illustrations-used where appropriate |
| Planning | ■ Researches topic<br>■ Lists ideas | ■ Sequences ideas<br>■ Identifies sources | ■ Considers the readers' needs in the planning |
| Sentences | ■ Begins sentences with capital letters<br>■ Ends sentences with periods | ■ Sentences are linked in a coherent order | ■ Uses variety in sentence structure to create effects |

**Figure 2.8.** Components of a rubric under development.

Once Pauline had descriptors for each level of learning—that is, a description of demonstrations at **I**deas, **C**onnections, and **E**xtensions—she compared additional pieces of completed work to search out other factors that contributed to judgments about the demonstrations of learning. She incorporated the additional qualities into the rubric until she was satisfied it was an accurate map of the learning she hoped to foster.

As teachers move along the continuum from novice to expert in ICE rubric construction, the portability of the tool will increase. Repeated practice in identifying and articulating the critical characteristics that distinguish **I**deas from **C**onnections and **E**xtensions levels of learning results in less reliance on rubrics, and more spur of the moment utility— a movement from rules to maxims.

## Differences Between Quantitative and Qualitative Rubrics

It is important to realize that the rubrics in quantitative and qualitative models have entirely different focuses. The focus in the former is number of correct responses, and in the latter, quality of responses. They are representative of different approaches to, and theories of, learning.

ICE rubrics differ significantly from most other rubrics because their descriptors are qualitative rather than quantitative. They describe the qualities, or definitive characteristics of the learning demonstration, rather than just the content or amount of work exhibited. Take the rubric shown in fig. 2.9 (designed for comprehension of French-as-a second-language) as a comparative example.

| Elements | Level 1 | Level 2 | Level 3 |
|---|---|---|---|
| Comprehension | ■ Includes some of the main ideas | ■ Includes most of the main ideas | ■ Includes all or almost all of the main ideas |
| Use of Language | ■ Uses some basic forms and vocabulary | ■ Uses most basic forms and vocabulary | ■ Uses all or almost all basic forms and vocabulary |

**Figure 2.9.** An example of a quantitative rubric for assessing second-language acquisition.

Notice the language of the rubric. The words *some, most, all,* and *almost* are indicative of the quantitative nature of the rubric and how it is to be used. Applying this particular rubric to students' oral or written translations would be a matter of the teacher (or student) counting the number of ideas and words that were correctly translated into French and the number of grammatical forms correctly employed. The results would be a quantitative analysis of the translation, enabling teachers to make some inferences about each student's current level of competency based on the number of correct responses.

While the resulting snap-shot of student learning does provide information about the student's current performance, the nature of the descriptors does not permit inferences to be made that would guide decisions about how to improve. The rubric allows for a quantitative analysis of the students' current levels of learning, but its use as a guide to improving that learning is limited. For that reason, the rubric will be more useful as a summative evaluation tool rather than as a formative aid for instructional and learning purposes.

Consider the rubric shown in fig. 2.10 as an alternative.

| Elements | Ideas | Connections | Extensions |
|---|---|---|---|
| Comprehension | ■ Direct one-to-one correspondence between the two languages | ■ General meaning of phrases is taken into account<br>■ Relates phrases to context | ■ Translation is true in tone, message, and spirit |
| Use of Language | ■ Verbatim translation | ■ Sequence of adjectives, adverbs, and nouns is adjusted in translation | ■ Uses appropriate English idiom equivalent<br>■ Creates tone appropriate to audience |

**Figure 2.10.** An example of a qualitative ICE rubric.

The ICE rubric in fig. 2.10 uses qualitative, rather than quantitative descriptors, to outline the characteristics of each stage of learning growth. The rubric describes the *type* of responses to expect as language learning develops, rather than the *number* of responses to expect. With ICE, the *quality* of French differs from stage to stage, increasing in fluency and tone. There is no such development of quality expressed in the quantitative rubric. It is, therefore, possible that the *quality* of

French demonstrated across the levels may be the same, with only the *number* of verbatim translations increasing from level to level.

Through the use of the ICE rubric, both the teacher and the student determine what the next steps toward learning growth are. The *qualities* of learning at various stages of development have been described in such a way that the teacher and students have a blueprint for learning development. No such blueprint exists as part of the quantitative rubric; it serves primarily as a summative yardstick.

So, when the new French teacher is informed that Mehdi is making Connections in his translations (fig. 2.10), she is immediately aware of the nature and quality of his language acquisition. Moreover, she has the information necessary to make decisions about where and how to continue the instructional process. Knowing that Mehdi is functioning in Level 2 (fig. 2.9) will give the teacher information about the number of errors being made, but cannot have as great an impact on instructional decisions. She will not have the necessary information about the nature of the errors being made.

After identifying and articulating the qualitative attributes of learning at progressive levels of competence, teachers are better able to interpret students' work and to design instructional strategies to facilitate growth toward the next level of competence. The implications for, and impact on, the development of teaching strategies carry across subject areas. Although math and science are typically viewed as "quantifiable subjects," there are parallel qualitative elements in learning development that influence instructional sequences and strategies. Consider the math rubric in fig. 2.11.

While the rubric shown in fig. 2.11 does describe different levels of achievement, the descriptors are largely quantitative. Notice words such as *some, most, all, sometimes, usually, always,* and *several, few,* and *none* used to describe the finished product. Using this rubric, teachers will be able to conduct an accurate count of procedures, steps, symbols, terms, and the like. Without accurate qualitative descriptors to characterize the demonstrations of learning, however, they will have little to help them determine where students' learning difficulties lie.

## Math Rubric*

| Category | Good | Better | Best |
|---|---|---|---|
| Core Content and Concepts | ■ Demonstrates limited understanding of some required concepts<br><br>■ Provides appropriate but incomplete explanations that incorporate some mathematical ideas and relationships | ■ Demonstrates general understanding of most required concepts<br><br>■ Provides appropriate and complete explanations that consistently incorporate mathematical ideas and relationships | ■ Demonstrates in-depth understanding of all required concepts<br><br>■ Provides appropriate and complete explanations of mathematical ideas and relationships, and incorporates the concepts in a variety of contexts |
| Reasoning and Applications | ■ Selects and applies some of the appropriate procedures and operations<br><br>■ Has several minor errors or omissions | ■ Selects and applies most of the appropriate procedures and operations<br><br>■ Has few minor errors or omissions | ■ Selects and applies almost all of the required procedures<br><br>■ Rare errors or omissions |
| Communication | ■ Provides justifications that have some clarity and precision<br><br>■ Uses some appropriate mathematical terms and symbols | ■ Provides justifications that are generally clear and precise<br><br>■ Uses mathematical terms and symbols that are usually appropriate | ■ Provides justifications that are clear and precise<br><br>■ Always uses a range of appropriate mathematical terms and symbols |
| Problem Solving | ■ Demonstrates limited understanding<br><br>■ Chooses and carries out some appropriate strategies<br><br>■ Sometimes arrives at accurate solutions | ■ Demonstrates a general understanding of the problem<br><br>■ Consistently chooses and carries out appropriate strategies<br><br>■ Usually accurate solutions | ■ Demonstrates a thorough understanding of the problem<br><br>■ Chooses and carries out innovative and appropriate strategies<br><br>■ Always accurate solutions |

**Figure 2.11.** Rubric for math, grades 1–8, using quantitative descriptors.

*Adapted from: The Ontario Curriculum grades 1–8 Mathematics, Ministry of Education and Training, 1997.

## Math Rubric*

| Element | Ideas | Connections | Extensions |
|---|---|---|---|
| Core Content and Concepts | ■ Completes basic content tasks<br>■ Defines, explains, and illustrates new concepts<br>■ Applies skills to familiar situations | ■ Combines procedures or structural concepts to solve two or more step problems<br>■ Applies content items across strands or between disciplines | ■ Uses concepts from one discipline to describe or illustrate another |
| Reasoning and Applications | ■ Makes valid observations based on available data<br>■ Records data using drawings, charts, or graphs | ■ Formulates generalizations and conjectures based on available data<br>■ Validates generalization based on logic or on counter-examples<br>■ Makes connections between known facts and the problem to be solved | ■ Validates his/her and others' thinking |
| Communication | ■ Uses mathematical terms, notations, and symbols to communicate ideas | ■ Links representations to connect information via tables, graphs, and symbols | |
| Problem Solving | ■ Clarifies the task<br>■ Selects relevant information<br>■ Approaches the problem with reason<br>■ Organizes information using tables, models, or patterns | ■ Applies explicit strategies (estimation, algorithms, working backwards, modeling)<br>■ Selects an appropriate strategy to develop a solution | ■ Makes observations or generalizations based on the solution<br>■ Relates or applies the solution or strategy to other domains |

*Adapted with permission from: L. E. C. Colgan and P. J. Harrison. "Rubrics: Their Purpose Is not to Drive You Crazy— It's to Drive Your Practice." The OAME Gazette 4, vol. 37 (June 1999): 7–13.

**Figure 2.12.** ICE rubric for math, grades 7–8, using qualitative descriptors.

In the alternative shown in fig. 2.12, the performance indicators, or critical elements of the assigned task, are specified and descriptors of performance at each of the ICE levels are provided. The rubric provides the teacher with a touchstone for assessing the learning being demonstrated through the assignment rather than solely on the number of correct responses.

The rubric "map" helps teachers determine the levels of learning development being demonstrated through the students' work. That, in turn, enables teachers to devise questions and arrange the learning environment in such a way as to challenge each student toward the next level of learning. That same "map" provides learners with the information they need to guide their own improvement.

In developing an appreciation for the communication and aesthetic elements of mathematics, teachers find ICE to be a useful tool in both teaching and assessing. The qualitative descriptors help teachers and learners focus on the developmental process of the learning rather than solely on the "right answers." Teachers then structure selected instructional activities to suit the developmental stages and enhance the practical, meaningful aspects of the subject.

Additionally, using ICE as a framework for math assessment in the classroom has positive effects on the way the subject is taught. It encourages teachers and students to consider math as part of their lives (**C**onnections and **E**xtensions) rather than just as sets of facts (**I**deas) to be mastered.

### Differences Between Checklists and ICE Rubrics

When first attempting to construct rubrics, there may be a tendency to systematically itemize the content of the work that is expected at each level of learning rather than to specify the quality of work that characterizes each level of learning development. As an example of the former, we present Phyllis's outline for her grade-five class's science project (fig. 2.13).

*       *       *

A *Good* project will have a:

- Hypothesis Statement
- List of Materials
- Method
- Conclusion
- Bibliography

In addition to the above, a *Better* project will also include:

- A description of how the project relates to what we learned in class and a project journal to describe what happened while you worked on your project

A *Great* project will have all the above elements plus:

- Suggestions of other ways of testing the same thing or an explanation of how the results of your experiment have changed your thinking

**Figure 2.13.** Quantitative outline for a science project.

In effect, Phyllis has created a quantitative checklist against which students can measure their projects, but only in terms of whether they have included the appropriate *number* of sections. What the checklist fails to do is delineate the characteristics that distinguish between projects that contain all the required components and those that demonstrate deep learning. A qualitative ICE rubric for the same project is shown in fig. 2.14.

Notice that while the format of the rubric has changed, the expectations about what students should include in the write-up of the experiment have not. What has changed is that now both the teacher and the students will become aware of the variations of expertise that may be demonstrated through the completion of each element of the experiment. What is more, there is now a clear blueprint, not only for assessment purposes, but for learning purposes as well. All class members now have the opportunity to respond to the challenges set out for them by the teacher.

| Elements | Ideas | Connections | Extensions |
|---|---|---|---|
| Comprehensiveness | ▪ Contains a hypothesis, list of materials, method, conclusion, bibliography | ▪ Elements are linked to each other in a consistent way; flow from one another | ▪ Elaborates on how experiment changed their thinking |
| Accuracy | ▪ All statements are accurate in terms of the experiment | ▪ Statements are qualified according to actual observations | ▪ Predictions are made about future experiments that might follow, and what their results might be |
| Presentation | ▪ Report is legible | ▪ Attention is paid to the needs of the reader | ▪ Creative ways of presenting results are attempted |

**Figure 2.14.** A qualitative ICE rubric for a science project.

## Summarizing Progress With Tests

It happens all the time. Two students from different classes compare their grades on the unit history test. Mike scored 89 percent and Sandy, a respectable, but lower, 75 percent. Mike spends a good part of the bus ride home feeling pretty good about himself for doing better than Sandy did in history. Sandy feels badly because she knows that she is a more competent student than her grade suggests.

Much of what testing is about is *quantifying* learning as a means of measuring learning *quality*. Since Mike has a significantly higher grade, he *must* have a better understanding of history than Sandy does. The general assumption is that high grades, by virtue of the fact they represent high numbers of correct responses, are indicative of high-quality learning. But what about the *inherent quality of the questions* that are used to elicit those responses? Using the ICE model, let us investigate some possibilities.

*       *       *

**A sample from Mike's history test:**

1. Provide a brief biography of Louis Riel.

2. What two skills were the Métis extremely good at?

3. How well did Riel also exhibit those skills?

4. What was another name for the North West?

5. Who was the Lieutenant Governor of the North West?

6. Where was Louis Riel educated? What did he study?

7. What was Riel's second act of resistance against the government?

8. Who headed Macdonald's Royal Commission to study the Métis issue?

9. Macdonald could not grant Riel amnesty, nor execute him. Why?

10. Who did Riel's government execute?

**A sample from Sandy's history test:**

1. What impact did the prevalent attitude of Canadians toward the Métis have in the development of the 1870 Rebellion?

2. What effect did the provisions that were made for the Métis have on their daily lives when the North West was sold?

3. What were the results of Macdonald's Royal Commission Study on the Métis issue?

Looking back over the two unit tests, it is easy to see the *qualitative* differences in the test questions that may have influenced the *quantitative* results. Mike's test required mastery of basic details, all **I**deas-level learning. While the questions from Sandy's test also required mastery of basic **I**deas, there was an expectation that learners would make **C**onnections among those ideas. Additionally, the opportunity was provided (for those who could) to make **E**xtensions, for students to take their answers beyond what had been covered in class. No such opportunities existed in the first test sample.

It is important to note that it is not always the case that students score higher grades on **I**deas-based tests and assignments than on those that invite **C**onnections and **E**xtensions. It is entirely possible, for example, that students may develop the capacity to discuss the intricacies of the Rebellion and have a deep appreciation and understanding of the material without being able to recall all of the details that were requested in Mike's test (**I**deas). Consider, too, that the format of Mike's test unnecessarily restricted students to demonstrations of lower-order learning.

Another caution is that the structure of questions may lead us to make erroneous assumptions about the quality of learning they elicit. On the surface, the first question from Mike's history test may look like an invitation to demonstrate deeper learning, but it requires nothing more than providing a compilation of facts (**I**deas).

## Tables of Specifications

The two history teachers, Giselle and Tron, were able to collaborate, analyze the content of their tests, and construct a new one that more accurately reflected their priorities for teaching and learning. They began the revisions by writing down what they agreed were the essential components of that unit in the history curriculum. Next, to ensure that there were opportunities for students to respond to a variety of question types, representative of different levels of learning for each of the essential components of the unit, they designed a grid (fig. 2.15).

| Topics | Ideas | Connections | Extensions |
|---|---|---|---|
| Louis Riel | | | |
| The Métis | | | |
| The Royal Commmission | | | |

**Figure 2.15.** First stage of developing a table of specifications: selecting main topics.

In effect, they created a table of specifications, of sorts, for that unit of history. It was a graphic depiction of the range of topics they wanted to cover in the test, and a challenge to them to develop questions that would invite some responses beyond the Ideas phase of learning.

Tables of specification are nothing more than a type of spreadsheet to help teachers design and review tests. They typically have course-content areas along one dimension and behaviors, question types, or learning levels along the other. The main purpose of these spreadsheets is to help teachers clarify the elements of any particular course that will be emphasized in a test. While this is particularly useful when two or more teachers of the same subject area are responsible for collaborating to design a single test, it is an equally valuable tool for teachers working on their own.

After the topics to be covered on the test are listed and the learning to be demonstrated in those content areas are selected, the next step is to determine the total number of marks for the test. In this case, Tron and Giselle had based their test grades out of 100 percent, and both agreed that it should remain that way.

Next, they had to decide how important each topic on the test was, relative to the others, and distribute the total number of marks on the test to reflect that. The table in fig. 2.16 shows the results of this discussion.

| Topics | Ideas | Connections | Extensions | Totals |
|---|---|---|---|---|
| Louis Riel | | | | 30 |
| The Métis | | | | 30 |
| The Royal Commission | | | | 40 |
| **Total** | | | | **100** |

**Figure 2.16.** Stage two in developing a table of specifications: mark distribution per topic.

The teachers both agreed that because the topic of the Royal Commission touched upon most of the other elements in the unit and was the topic they spent the most class time on, it should be the most heavily weighted of the three.

Now, all that was left to decide was the number of marks to allot for each cell representing the different levels of learning. They agreed that they wanted their students to have a comprehensive appreciation of the situation leading up to the Rebellion and were less interested in their ability to recall the "bits and pieces" Ideas. Thus, they reserved the greatest number of marks for Connections and Extensions.

After the discussions and arithmetic juggling were complete, the final table looked a little different from the initial one, but still reflected the teachers' content and learning outcome priorities (fig. 2.17).

| Topics | Ideas | Connections | Extensions | Totals |
|---|---|---|---|---|
| Louis Riel | 10 | 15 | | 25 |
| The Métis | 10 | 20 | | 30 |
| The Royal Commission | 10 | 15 | 20 | 45 |
| **Total** | **30** | **50** | **20** | **100** |

**Figure 2.17.** Final stage of table construction: allocation of marks to levels of learning.

As a result of this work, the teachers became fully aware of what their teaching and learning priorities of this unit of history were. They were then able to devise questions for the test that were compatible with the blueprint they had set for themselves. What's more, if they chose to, they could share the table with students to give them an indication of the type of learning that was expected to be demonstrated on the test.

\*　　\*　　\*

Shelly, a new grade-ten science teacher, had a different, but related need for a table of specifications. She had been offered the use of another teacher's test for the physics unit she was preparing on Electrical Applications. Uncertain about whether or not the test was reflective of her expectations for learning in that unit, she began by noting the content areas covered on the test:

- Series and parallel circuits
- Static and current electricity
- Measurement

Then, she made note of the grading weight for each content area and found that the questions on Measurement accounted for the largest proportion of the test's marks. Next, she wanted to see what kind of learning was required for a student to do well on the test. To do that, she had to make a judgment about the type of learning required by each of the test questions. Shelly thought a chart would help (fig. 2.18).

| Topics | Ideas | Connections | Extensions | Totals |
|--------|-------|-------------|------------|--------|
| Series and Parallel Circuits | 8 | 10 | | 18 |
| Static and Current Electricity | 4 | 6 | | 10 |
| Measurement | 22 | | | 22 |
| **Total** | **34** | **16** | | **50** |

**Figure 2.18.** Table of specifications to help determine suitability of an existing test.

Shelly was able to determine that not only was Measurement the primary focus of this test, but that it seemed to have been designed to test basic knowledge—Ideas-level learning—since that was the only type of question on the test for that topic. It also became evident that students would need a more developed understanding of circuits (Connections level) to do well on that portion of the test.

Through this quick, yet thorough process, Shelly had created a table of specifications that helped her analyze the existing test to determine its suitability for assessing learning in her classroom. Additionally, the opportunity existed for Shelly to evaluate the quality of the questions on the test. Were they constructed to encourage demonstrations of learning? Were the difficult questions difficult because of the complexity of learning required to answer them, or were they difficult because of the complexity of the structure of the question?

Shelly must now decide whether or not the existing test is representative of the expectations she has for her students' learning of the content they covered in her class. She must also decide if, and how, to create opportunities for students to demonstrate Extensions in their learning, if they are capable of doing so.

If Shelly was reviewing a selected-response test she would probably choose to analyze both the questions *and* the selection options of each multiple-choice question. She knows that careful construction of the test may help to simplify the interpretation of results later. If the items are constructed so that incorrect options represent typical response-errors at varying levels of learning growth, she will be able to determine not only the number of correct responses, but also gain insight into the level of learning that led to errors. Building ICE-based responses into the answer options affords teachers the opportunity to make instructional decisions based on qualitative as well as quantitative results.

It is not always necessary, or appropriate, to test beyond Ideas-level learning. There are many instances when it is vital to ascertain how well the fundamentals have been acquired, purely and simply. The critical factor is for teachers to be acutely aware of exactly what type of learning they are assessing each time they choose to assess.

Teachers who have not developed proficiency in a given subject area will face challenges implementing ICE—they may have difficulty articulating the Connections and identifying possibilities for Extensions. Teachers with expert, subject-specific knowledge have the benefit of appreciating the subtle nuances of the subject matter and the markers that distinguish one level of learning competence from the next. That is not to say that using ICE is limited to subject-area specialists. However, it may mean that teaching needs to evolve into a more collaborative practice than it currently is in some schools.

## Grading and Reporting Progress

It is important to appreciate that many teachers *and* administrators may not have reconciled, for themselves, the essential differences between qualitative and quantitative characteristics of learning. The lapse may arise from well-intentioned attempts to accurately report and document learning achievement. Often, quantitative measures such as letter grades, rankings, and percentages are so intricately associated with demonstrations of learning that the qualitative distinctions between the demonstrations are absorbed into them. An example might help to illustrate the point:

When one teacher was asked to explain the difference between work that is deemed to be "average" and that which is "fair," he replied that average work is C-level (65–75 percent) and fair work is D-level (55–64 percent). He defined the caliber of the work by the quantitative grade rather than by the specific qualitative characteristics of work at each level.

The quantitative values are important for students to know for administrative purposes and for documenting achievement, but students' learning could be much better guided by descriptions of the qualities that "fair," "average," and "good" work exhibit. In fact, by using only numerical values, the communication from the teacher only tells the student where he or she is in terms of grading. Numerical values provide no insight to what the next steps toward improvement might be.

Learning can be enhanced through the assessment process when teachers and peers share qualitative feedback on students' work. The learner then has the opportunity to reflect on the feedback before planning for the next steps in the learning process. As demonstrated in earlier chapters, the use of ICE rubrics and tables of specifications facilitate these processes.

ICE provides a framework for understanding, structuring, and assessing learning development. When approached from that perspective, generating marks through use of the ICE model is not unlike generating marks using other models. The fundamental difference is that the ICE framework helps to describe the learning it is helping to assess. Those descriptions enable teachers to make decisions about next steps for teaching and learning as well as assign grades for reporting purposes.

Most teachers who use ICE establish marking parameters early on: typically, Ideas-level demonstrations are set as a basic minimum requirement for success, and movement along the novice to expert continuum typically results in higher grades being assigned. Those same distinctions can also be made in what are typically viewed as the more *objective* courses.

Teachers respond to qualitative differences in answers to math problems every time they correct homework and tests. In many cases, however, the final numerical score on a math test is a direct reflection of the number of correct answers, regardless of the qualitative root of the errors. It may be entirely possible for two students to receive similar quantitative scores and yet be in different stages of qualitative learning development if test results are based solely on the generation of correct final answers. Offering qualitative feedback also helps students learn more about their learning growth.

*   *   *

Consider the results of two arithmetic quizzes that Mark, a primary teacher, had to consider (fig. 2.19a–b).

Note that both Jill and Jack earned the same grade on the quiz, even making errors in the same problems. Yet, the error patterns of their responses indicate a significant difference in their learning. Jill makes a consistent Ideas-level error in adding 7 and 6 to get 12. Jack on the other hand, fails to do any regrouping as he adds—an indication that he may not yet have made the Connections necessary to carry.

The results of the quiz yield two types of information for Mark to consider—the quantitative score and the qualitative demonstrations of learning development. Both sets of information are necessary for him to make decisions about approaches to teaching and to selection of follow-up tasks for each student. Analyzing the *quality* of the mistakes, as well as the number of mistakes *before* devising teaching strategies, addresses the weaknesses in learning demonstrated in those answers.

**Monday Morning Quiz**

Name Jill     7/10

| | | |
|---|---|---|
| 1) 67 +30 = 97 | 2) 123 +456 = 579 | 3) 37 +46 = 82 (circled) |
| 4) 321 +568 = 889 | 5) 269 +675 = 934 (circled) | 6) 83 +14 = 97 |
| 7) 432 +267 = 699 | 8) 52 +43 = 95 | 9) 726 +52 = 778 |
| | 10) 26 +37 = 62 (circled) | |

a.

**Monday Morning Quiz**

Name Jack     7/10

| | | |
|---|---|---|
| 1) 67 +30 = 97 | 2) 123 +456 = 579 | 3) 37 +46 = 73 (circled) |
| 4) 321 +568 = 889 | 5) 269 +675 = 834 (circled) | 6) 83 +14 = 97 |
| 7) 432 +267 = 699 | 8) 52 +43 = 95 | 9) 726 +52 = 778 |
| | 10) 26 +37 = 53 (circled) | |

b.

**Figure 2.19a–b.** Primary arithmetic quizzes.

Supplementing the quantitative score with notations about what the error patterns indicate about learning development provides a blueprint for future teaching and learning. Linking grading to learning *quality* (in this case, to demonstrations of higher-level arithmetic functions), helps do the same. A time-honored way of attempting to link grading to learning quality is to weight the more involved questions more heavily—say, five points instead of two. Unfortunately, the overall effects on the test results depend more on the variability in the marks earned than on the weighting of the items.

\*    \*    \*

David, who teaches business courses at the secondary-school level, has been known to quip, "Evaluation I don't mind. It's marking I hate." David's statement encapsulates the ambiguity that many teachers feel as they attempt to reconcile the different purposes of assessment. In the first instance, David refers to assessment as it is used to enhance student learning. It is the exchange of ideas and qualitative feedback that leads to improved understanding and helps learners answer the question: Where do I go from here?

The second part of his statement refers to that component of the assessment process that involves documenting learning achievement for reporting purposes. It usually requires teachers to produce a percentage or letter grade to represent the outcome of the learning. Grading is done primarily for administrative purposes with priorities on record keeping and documenting achievement. Teachers often experience more reticence about the process of assigning final grades than they do when offering formative assessment, because their priorities in assessing differ from administrators'. Teachers are more concerned with improving learning than with documentation and record keeping.

Despite the fact that teachers' primary focus is on their students' learning and growth, they are still required to contribute to the documentation of learning achievement through grading. Those formally reported grades have traditionally been interpreted as representations of the end results of learning. That connotation of finality is something that many would like to avoid especially those among us who regard learning as an ongoing process of growth and development. The ICE model serves as a bridge between the classic summative grading traditions and some teachers' preferences for critical, formative assessment that fosters ongoing learning.

David and others have devised grading schemes that reflect their beliefs about the developmental nature of learning while respecting the institution's need for reporting and documenting student achievement. The ICE model provides the framework to assess learning as a progression from novice through expert—from Ideas through Extensions—and still fits nicely into administrative expectations about grading.

In David's class, Ideas are considered to be a possession; something students have. As such, Ideas-level learning represents the basic, minimum requirement for a passing grade in his classes. Students must be able to demonstrate that they have developed a facility with the fundamental concepts, language, and theories of advertising.

Because Connections-level learning requires that students demonstrate the relationships among the basic concepts and previous learning with the course material, those learning demonstrations are more highly valued than Ideas-level learning. As a result of those values, the grades awarded for Connections-level learning are higher than those for Ideas-level demonstrations.

The qualitative nature of the descriptors in David's rubrics encourage his students to demonstrate a learning proficiency beyond simply responding (correctly) to fact-based questions. One result is that students begin to appreciate their learning as evidence of growth along a mastery continuum that spans from novice to expert. The learning continuum helps to convey that opportunities for learning continue apart from the classroom experience. Students come to expect and understand that their learning will continue after the formal course experience is over.

Nonetheless, the students, their parents, and David all understand that they are functioning within a primarily summative, quantitative world where letter grades and numerical scores are the reality of everyday life. That being the case, David's students conduct student-led conferences as a way of sharing their progress with their parents. Through learning portfolios, the students offer tangible, practical evidence of their learning. They, and their parents, develop an appreciation that the grades reflect the quality of their learning rather than a tabulation of right and wrong answers. In a student-led conference, the parents of 16-year-old Chloe asked why she was working so hard in this course and not so hard in her others. She replied: "I can't believe it! I'm learning stuff in school!"

The invitation to make Extensions, and the value that is placed on attempts to do so, encourage students to regard assessment results only as the most recent snapshots of their continuing progress along the learning continuum. The framework of ICE does a good job of putting learning in perspective over time, helping students view assessment results as indicators of continuing growth rather than as a summation of an end result.

\*     \*     \*

Before report cards go home at mid-term, Mr. P.'s elementary school students prepare to conduct their student-led conferences. They compile personal learning portfolios with examples of first attempts, second tries, and final products as a means of demonstrating to their parents just how far they have come in their learning. Students also use the occasion to explain, in their own terms, how and what they have learned, and how that learning will be recorded on report cards. The process ensures that each student develops an understanding and appreciation of the pattern and development of their own learning.

An additional component of the conference is that students share their plans for continued improvement with their parents. They can begin to outline specific strategies for learning success rather than just make plans to increase their grade by, say, 5 percent because ICE contributes the language and the framework for them to do that. They can talk in terms of additional ways to use new learning and about plans to put new twists on old learning.

*    *    *

Sharing rubrics and expectations with students means that everyone becomes aware of what types of demonstrations are necessary at each level of learning development, and of what measures might be taken for improvement. In these ways, ICE serves as a framework for students to develop skills in self- and peer-assessment. After time and experience, students will begin to apply the principles of ICE, without construction of formal rubrics, to their own and others' work. Independent and non-teacher-initiated instances of students' use of ICE mean that students are well on their way to developing self-assessment and independent learning skills.

## A Final Note About Grading

Grading usually involves the application of rules: combining results to produce a single summary label. For example, all the scores on class work are added and combined with the scores on tests to make a final score that is then translated into a grade.

Using more growth-oriented, individualized models hampers this objectified approach to grading. It allows individuals to produce work that may differ markedly from that produced by others in the same class.

The use of rubrics helps with the combining task by enabling the teacher and students to use an identical scale to assess work that is different. The growth model helps further by placing students on a continuum of learning.

The translation to either a criterion or normative scheme can then be made on the basis of common information on learners. David, for example, who must use a percentage scale to report grades in his school, simply uses ICE rubrics to reflect ranges of grades which he then discusses with each student. Mr. P. uses student-led conferences with parents as a support to the report card that demands a single "level" classification. Parents see the quality of the work their child produces in a context of curricular expectations. This richness of information in turn makes the reported grade understandable in a way that the bare-bones description on the report itself could not hope to communicate. Bob W. uses his rubrics as occasions to elaborate on his students' strengths and weaknesses: he then translates all of this information into a grade that is usually interpreted normatively at the college level even when criteria have been used to establish the achievement level.

## Sharing ICE With Learners

Sharing the framework of ICE with learners affords them the opportunity to appreciate the developmental nature of their own learning. Once that has been acknowledged and fostered, they can begin to develop strategies to improve their learning by determining logical progressions toward learning growth. They can then begin to develop an appreciation for the variations in the quality of their own learning.

As with other subject areas, the way in which teachers explain the fundamental concepts of ICE and its uses has a lasting effect on students' understanding of the model and, consequently, on their ability to use it to its best advantage.

*       *       *

John, a teacher in the Business Department of a community college, was grappling with ways to explain the variations in the quality of work he had received from his students that would make sense and help them understand the resulting spectrum of grades on the last class assignment. The assignment had been to analyze a case study. John chose the following approach:

> *Let me see: It was as if the case study was a broken toaster. Some of you went through the case and sort of said, 'Yup, the toaster's broken.' You pointed out all the parts in the case study that contributed to the problem. You were right and you stopped there.*

> *Another group of you agreed that the toaster was broken and you went on to say WHY it was broken and maybe even said what effect the broken parts had on the rest that wasn't broken.*

> *A very small group of you said, 'Yup, the toaster's broken. Here's how it's broken, how it got broken, AND how to fix it.' Now THAT'S a complete analysis.*

In many respects, John's after-the-fact, broken toaster analogy reflects the same kind of qualitative analysis that is involved in an ICE rubric:

- *Yup, the toaster's broken* (**I**deas): Fundamental elements of dysfunction are identified.
- *The toaster's broken, and here's why* (**C**onnections): The relationships between factors are identified; cause-and-effect inferences are made.
- *The toaster's broken; here's why, and here's how to fix it* (**E**xtensions): Extrapolations are made from the course content to the novel situation of the case study; modifications are suggested and viable solutions to the problem situations are proposed.

John's ability to articulate the characteristics of "Good," "Better," and "Wow" case analyses came after he had the opportunity to read the completed assignments. He took the time to reflect on the differences while he was engaged in the assessment process and has since begun to preface the case study assignment with the broken toaster analogy. He feels confident that the descriptors offered provide his students with a framework for high quality work without the pitfalls of "giving them the answers." Knowing what the differences are between **I**deas, **C**onnections, and **E**xtensions does not mean that every student will be able to make them.

$$* \quad * \quad *$$

In another example of demystifying the assessment process for and with students, Bob involved his class of graduate students in the development of a rubric for assessing the class presentations they were about to give. In preparation for the task, Bob introduced the ICE model by taking just a few minutes to distinguish between **I**deas, **C**onnections, and **E**xtensions levels of learning. Once the students understood the fundamental concepts, they set to apply them to their upcoming presentations.

After discussion in small groups, the class, as a whole, agreed on the essential elements of the upcoming presentations. The students initially determined that there were four critical elements that merited assessment: clarity, knowledge, application of the presentation topic, and materials.

By asking each group to focus on a single element of the presentation, Bob continued using the discussion groups for student-generated descriptors representative of each level of ICE.

After collecting and reviewing the students' single-element rubrics, Bob discovered that the knowledge element was not distinct. Knowledge was represented in different ways in each of the other components, so it was omitted as an independent element but incorporated into the others in the final draft of the rubric. When compiled, the groups' work looked something like the chart shown in fig. 2.20.

The whole process took about twenty minutes of class time. It took approximately one hour of Bob's after-class time to compile the groups' work to produce the final rubric. Bob wrote them up exactly as they had been received with the exception of incorporating the "knowledge" category into the other elements. He then assigned an evaluative label to each column (OK, Better, and Awesome) to help the students gain a sense of what each of the ICE levels represented in terms of learning and skill demonstration.

The students then examined Bob's compilation and agreed that it captured what they all believed to be important about their presentations. The end result was that each member of the class had

| Elements | Ideas | Connections | Extensions |
|---|---|---|---|
| Clarity | ■ Makes accurate statements about the topic<br>■ Terminology and concepts are clearly defined<br>■ Logical, coherent presentation | ■ Appropriate illustrations<br>■ Responds to questions<br>■ Connects ideas to each other<br>■ Connects concepts to classroom situations<br>■ Helps audience make connections to their own situations | ■ Extrapolates understanding to new situations<br>■ Relates the presentation to other parts of the course/program |
| Application | ■ Offers a basic description of applicability of the material<br>■ Uses textbook generated examples to demonstrate applicability<br>■ Detailed explanation of applicability to the data set | ■ Prepares audience to decide on applicability to the field<br>■ Presentation is interesting and relevant to students' interests | ■ Critical thinking is demonstrated by presenter<br>■ Audience participates and demonstrates applicability to their own practice<br>■ Applies material to unique situations |
| Materials | ■ Handouts include:<br> • Resources<br> • Definitions<br>■ Useful<br>■ Approachable<br>■ Diversity of presentation styles<br>■ Clear and consise | ■ Presentation refers to materials<br>■ Flows in a logical pattern<br>■ Provides questions for reflection | ■ Provides resources for further exploration (e.g., web sites, related research organizations) |
| **Evaluation** | **OK** | **Better** | **Awesome** |

**Figure 2.20.** ICE rubric for class presentations.

more of a personal stake in, and ownership of, the process. They knew what their peers and the instructor valued and what was necessary for them to do to demonstrate their learning.

The rubrics were used to offer feedback to each of the presenters. By checking off the individual descriptors that applied to individual presentations, and using the ample room on the page to provide anecdotal comments, each presenter was offered constructive and supportive input. Bob had the responsibility of assigning a final, numerical grade based on both the descriptors that had been checked off and the anecdotal comments.

Bob intentionally did not assign grading values to each of the three demonstration levels. It has been his experience that when grade values are included as part of the rubric, students tend to focus on them rather than on the descriptors of learning associated with each level of growth.

*　　*　　*

Mary-Lou, an art teacher, had a similar experience when she involved her high-school class in the rubric design process. Like many teachers, she had an assessment scheme that she had relied on before. Unfortunately, the predominantly quantitative nature of the system was not helping her students develop as artists. Her students could infer how they were doing by the grade they received on the assignment. But there was no way for them to easily determine the steps they needed to take for improvement that did not involve time-consuming writing on the teacher's part, or informal one-on-one meetings after the fact.

The marks for the Cool Palette Painting exercise were based on three components, and the original assessment scheme was as follows:

| | |
|---|---|
| Use of Cool Palette/Sketch | /10 |
| Unity | /10 |
| Brush Technique | /10 |

The grading grid had always been shared with the students (fig. 2.21).

| Elements | <6<br>Unacceptable | 6 – 6.4<br>Fair | 6.5 – 7.4<br>Average | 7.5 – 8.4<br>High Level | 8.5<br>Outstanding |
|---|---|---|---|---|---|
| Sketch | | | | | |
| Unity | | | | | |
| Brush Technique | | | | | |

**Figure 2.21.** An example of a grading grid: a quantitative approach.

Inevitably, students wanted Mary-Lou to supply them with examples of fair- , average- , and high-level work. In short, the quantitative grid did not supply them with enough information to guide their learning and skill development.

Through comparisons of art work and group discussion, the class and Mary-Lou collaborated to produce a qualitative rubric to help guide skill development and self- , peer- , and teacher-assessment of the assignment (fig. 2.22).

Because she took the students through the process of rubric design in much the same way that was outlined on pages 31-33, the collaborative process in Mary-Lou's class took considerably longer than in Bob's. The unanticipated benefit from the experience in Mary-Lou's class was that the students developed a comprehensive appreciation of the interrelated elements of art. They began to develop a critical eye based on those elements rather than on idiosyncratic tastes and loosely defined criteria. In short, the investment of time was worth it.

The framework of ICE encourages "front-ending assessment." That means that expectations and parameters are delineated at the outset of every learning task. Front-ending assessment takes time and care. Investing the time early on in the process usually results in spending less time grappling with subjectivity and criteria issues after the fact.

| Elements | Ideas | Connections | Extensions |
|---|---|---|---|
| Sketch | ■ A preliminary sketch of the work is provided on tissue and transferred onto white card | ■ Shading on the sketch indicates light and dark areas and textures to be included in the final work | ■ All compositional details have been addressed<br>■ The sketch is complete enough to use as a painting blueprint |
| Unity | ■ All colors are from a cool palette<br>■ Pure colors are used throughout | ■ Mixed colors are of equal intensity<br>■ There is evidence of palette-mixed, rather than work-surface mixed paint<br>■ Black and white are used to create a variety of shades of gray | ■ Toned colors are combined to create depth, volume, and a sense of texture |
| Brush Technique | ■ Brush selection is appropriate for medium used | ■ A variety of brush sizes and textures is used for visual interest | ■ Brush strokes used create texture, volume, and depth |

**Figure 2.22.** This example shows a qualitative rubric, using the ICE approach.

Teachers have indicated that it takes a high level of confidence to share the use of ICE with their students. The confidence borne of subject-area expertise goes a long way toward facilitating the process of identifying the finer points and nuances of learning development. Teachers without subject-area expertise feel an ever higher level of risk if there are few opportunities to collaborate with others to generate rubrics and generally help map students' learning.

A Final Note About Sharing ICE With Students

It also takes a high level of confidence on the part of teachers to relinquish control that some believe exists in a predominantly **I**deas-based classroom. Encouraging learners to make **C**onnections and **E**xtensions involves an element of uncertainty. Perhaps it is precisely that uncertainty about where learning can lead that some students find so exhilarating!

## Students' Reactions to ICE

The students in Mr. P.'s grade five/six class get particularly excited when they have been able to make Extensions in their learning. They have coined the phrase "I ICEd it!" to acknowledge to themselves, and the class, that they have managed to make that extra leap in learning that gets them beyond being in command of facts and data to changing the way they view the world— even if it is in a very small way. They have come to appreciate the difference between knowing bits and pieces of information and using those bits and pieces (Ideas) to create something new.

*　　*　　*

Groups of three or four of Mr. P.'s students got together to talk about using ICE in their classroom and what it means to the way they learn:

> *I like ICE. It challenges you to do more and to think and lets people be recognized for doing things.*

> *It makes me create new things. I like to be the one to think of something new. It doesn't always have to be the teacher. It's always nice to surprise a teacher with something they hadn't expected.*

They all seemed to be energized when talking about the positive effects the model has had on their learning, so the question was raised about their plans for next year, when they might be in a classroom with a teacher unfamiliar with ICE. Lydia's immediate response was:

> *ICE is really easy to learn and really easy to tell people about. I'd explain it to the teacher and I'm sure she'd use it. Even if she didn't, I could still do it myself, but it would be better if the whole class did it together.*

Eileen had a different approach:

> *I'd wait a while to see what the teacher is like. Sometimes you can tell a teacher is an ICE teacher even though they don't know it. They make sure you learn a lot, not just know stuff. They make learning fun and they do things that you're interested in. They help you use what you're learning for the things they know you like.*

Sentiments like these were expressed by students repeatedly. Regardless of whether their teachers used ICE or another model of assessment, students liked knowing what teachers' expectations for learning and learning demonstrations were. Moreover, they all preferred the challenges inherent in requirements compelling them to make personal meaning of their learning rather than just master facts.

*   *   *

Stephen, a high-school student in David's advertising class, was part of a focus group set up to discuss learning within an ICE framework. He summed it up this way:

> *Using ICE for learning and for assessing isn't easier than the other, more traditional ways where you count up right and wrong answers, but that's OK. I learn a lot more because I'm so much more involved.*

The engagement in the process that Stephen talks about comes from what students interpret as the teacher's respect for their capacity to do more than just master facts. In turn, the students developed an appreciation for the way they were learning in David's class. Some of them shared their views in these terms:

> *Mr. N. expects you to make **C**onnections. In a lot of other classes, it's just the **I**deas stuff and the teachers don't get past that level. And it's the **C**onnections and **E**xtensions that are the exciting part of learning!*

> *ICE is Mr. N.'s way of helping us interpret what we're learning. He sees whether we know the basic information (**I**deas) he's taught, if we can relate it to other things (**C**onnections), and if we can expand on that to higher levels and to our other work.*

> *In a lot of classes, you just memorize stuff, spit it out, and forget it. Here, we get more involved with what we're doing. I know now that if I'm able to **C**onnect and **E**xtend, then, obviously, I've learned.*

When the conversation turned to the quality of learning being done, all the students agreed: when there is an opportunity or an expectation that students will make personal meaning of the learning through forming **C**onnections and going through the AHA! phase of **E**xtensions, the learning lasts longer.

> *In some classes where you just learn the "stuff," I'll remember it for the test, because I've done a good job of memorizing the pieces the teacher said were important, but if I don't have anything to hang it on, I lose it. Then I look back and wonder: what did I learn?*

> *In this course, I know what I have to do if I want to do well. In other courses, you don't know that. All you know is that if you'd gotten more right answers your mark would have been higher. This way, you can self-assess. Here, you know how well you know your stuff. In this class, Mr. N.'s not so much interested in the **I**deas you know, but what you did with those **I**deas.*

# CHAPTER 3

# The Versatility of ICE

The examples provided throughout this text illustrate the wide range of applications for ICE across the curriculum and across demonstrations of learning. Proponents of the model are convinced that ICE can be used in every instance where there is an opportunity to assess learning growth, both formally and informally, regardless of the subject matter or the demonstration venue.

## Across Curriculum Areas

Examples included in earlier chapters demonstrate that ICE can be used successfully as both a teaching and assessment tool in areas as diverse as graphic arts and mathematical problem solving and from kindergarten through graduate school. Here, teachers share their perspectives on using ICE in areas of special interest to them.

### Drama and Music

After a very brief introduction to ICE and a few examples of what learning at each of the three developmental stages might look like in other subject areas, Len, a high-school drama teacher, was immediately able to relate it to how students demonstrate learning in his classes.

In clarifying the model for himself, Len contended that the Ideas level is most often represented by students' abilities to accurately describe and demonstrate the foundations of theater: to demonstrate techniques such as mime, tableau, and focus level in the drama classes and skills such as finger placement, sight-reading, and accuracy in the music classes. Len believes that movement toward the Connections phase of learning development occurs when students go beyond description and demonstration to apply those techniques to create something new, first in a structured environment, then in an improvised one. He describes Extensions-level learning this way:

> *The people who do reach Extensions are people who use and understand the concepts and the use of those concepts and you see that flow over into the way they behave in general; it's become part of who they are. So that when they walk into a room you see them using those communication skills. You see them using problem-solving skills. You see them using group skills. And in drama, those are the three major skills you're trying to develop. So you see those skills in the classroom, but then you also see them in the Student Common. It's in a completely different context and they can do it because they understand the implications of the skills elsewhere. The skills have become such a big part of who they are now that they can make the transfer.*

When asked to explain differences between what some people refer to as raw talent and learned skills, Len considered that

> *...everyone sees the world differently and that 'different' way of seeing may allow those kids to make the jump from Connections to Extensions a little more easily. They've been able to do the 'aha' thing because of the way they view the world. Our job, as teachers, is to set up the environment in such a way as to help the others develop their ways of seeing the world.*

He did have a few cautionary words:

> *Having technical ability is one thing, but if you can't make it your own and extend it beyond that technical first step, that technical perfection might be just Ideas-level learning. It's the people who can convey the emotion, can convey the character as well as be technically accurate who are moving along the spectrum toward Extensions. Not all people recognize that there's something beyond technical perfection.*

One of the reasons why Len liked the idea of using ICE is that the model helps safeguard against comparison grading. As in many other curriculum areas, there can be a tendency in the arts for teachers to identify the most technically gifted student in the class as the standard of comparison for other learners. Grading then becomes a matter of determining the degree to which the other class members approach that level of competence. The method is limiting for everyone involved. Len argues that it does little, if anything, to help the gifted student develop further, and it conveys nothing more to the others than "This is great, and you're not here yet." Providing descriptors of learning within the ICE framework, in terms of the qualities that characterize development, helps to ensure that judgments made about learning are based on objective criteria, and that all students have a plan for learning clearly set out.

*   *   *

## Trades and Technology

The physical skills acquired in the shop classroom parallel the developmental growth patterns exhibited in other types of learning. According to Tom, a high-school shop teacher, using ICE as a framework for assessing skill development makes perfect sense. Tom described what he viewed as some of the broad **I**deas-level learning: knowing and following safety protocols, steps for operating the machinery, basic math, and knowing and describing essential characteristics of various building materials—all basic, but essential knowledge and skills. **C**onnections were described as occurring when students combined some of those skills and knowledge to construct a physical product. **E**xtensions were described as the full production of a student-generated design.

On a smaller scale, Tom contends that every finished product and demonstration of equipment use can be assessed and described using the ICE framework. He used facility with the band saw as an example:

> *Kids who are in the initial stage of learning tend to fidget at the saw, reviewing step by step the procedure they're to follow and the protocols set out. They may measure and remeasure the wood they're about to cut. The kids who have made the **C**onnections will condense some of the steps of the protocol and operating procedure and will measure the distance from the blade to the edge rather than measure the wood.*

Tom went on to explain that being able to successfully condense the process by collapsing steps into each other means that productivity goes up—something employers are ready to reward! One way that Tom conveys the importance of the quality of the students' finished products is by linking to real-world criteria. He asks students to gauge how much they would be willing to pay for each finished piece of work if top-quality workmanship can fetch $10.00. Through this method of self- and peer-assessment, the students are able to evaluate each piece of work, in this case covered wooden boxes, using qualitative criteria. The exercise reinforces the importance of quality and compels the students to critically evaluate each characteristic of form and workmanship. They develop a greater appreciation for even, jointed edges over nailed edges, for snug-fitting lids more than either loose or tight ones, and for smooth edges more than rough ones. Moreover, they become acutely aware of the requisite skills to produce each characteristic.

It is interesting to note the level of subject-area expertise that helps inform Tom's teaching. In most instances, teachers can ascertain at a glance where on the learning spectrum any particular student is. In some instances, Tom, himself, need not be anywhere near a student to make that assessment. Hissing sounds coming from the welding area indicate that too much oxygen is coming through the valve; a high-pitched whine from the band saw means that the angle of the cut has been misjudged—both signs of novices at work.

\*       \*       \*

Christina teaches computer applications to adults. Formal-learning assessment is not part of her workshops. She does, however, have a good grasp of what, and how well, her students are learning by using ICE as a tool for interpreting learners' behaviors, comments, and questions.

Like Tom, Christina shares the perception that the more novice students are likely to follow protocols scrupulously, step by step, without shortcuts. They also tend to ask fact-based questions (Ideas level) that she can typically answer with a yes/no or short-response answer. Students with more highly developed expertise are more likely to ask what she refers to as "multiple-level questions" that require more involved responses from her, an indication that they are beginning to make Connections. The students who are able to ask those types of questions are also the ones who are able to do a single assigned task in a variety of ways—they've made some of the Connections that allow them to make those inferences.

*   *   *

## Sports and Physical Education

Acquisition of physical skills appears to follow patterns similar to the learning development required in academic subjects. There is a well-defined skill progression that is based on qualitative, rather than quantitative, measures leading learners from novice through to expert levels.

One such example is given by Lesley, a high-school basketball coach, who used passing as an illustrative example of how ICE can be used to help players become better at what they do. She observed that novice players tend to be quite robotic in their passing motions, largely because they tend to rehearse each step of pass mechanics and consciously call it to mind the instant before they perform the motion (Ideas). While the result is a well-planned and perhaps technically good pass, the result may not stand up well in a game situation. Players with a little more expertise are able to pass on the run; they have managed to condense some of the steps to create more fluid movement and are able to combine the momentum from their run with their pass mechanics to achieve results (Connections). Beyond that are the players who "see the floor." These players have developed a sense of the game, and a sense of their own presence and other team members to such a degree that they are able to create "no-look passes," anticipating the position of the receiver even before she/he reaches it (Extensions). They can lead others into the ball. Lesley was quick to point out the fluidity of motion is an indication that much of what occurs is not at the conscious level; the players have ceased having to visualize their moves. They have moved beyond the fundamental rules of the mechanics, adapting them into who they are as players.

Articulating the skill-qualities that players at each level of development are likely to display means that Lesley can plan strategies for helping her players improve from one stage of development to the next. She noted that telling players to make more of their passes or sink more of their free throws does nothing to help them improve as players. What they need are specific markers that indicate improvement, and ICE helps by providing the framework.

Most sports skills can be assessed and taught in a similar way regardless of what the desired quantitative outcomes are. Swimming farther faster might be the ultimate outcome, but increasing efficiency through proper mechanics (a qualitative process) will be the method of choice for instructional purposes.

## Across Products of Learning

In their own learning development, some teachers are discovering a new freedom that arises from using the ICE model. It is a freedom from content sameness. They have discovered that the framework of ICE affords the structure and basis to make sound, objective judgments about each individual student's learning without the need to have every student demonstrate his or her learning in exactly the same way. Why is that important? Jim explains it this way:

> At the end of the course, what I want my students to do is to extend their learning, frame it, contextualize it in who they are and how it's important to them. And that's why I can't predict, and don't want to suppose that I can choose for them, the context in which they can extend what they've learned in my class. The ultimate cost of NOT affording students the opportunity to demonstrate their learning in ways that are meaningful to them is dependency. What I'm really looking for is the extent to which the momentum in learning is taken over by the student, so that I can step out of their learning-loop; so that the learning momentum now comes from them.

Using course outlines, learning outcomes as guideposts, and ICE as a framework to describe the expectations for learning at each level of development, Jim is confident that both he and his students can assess the quality of learning demonstrated through each of the products he receives as final projects, each different from the next.

Jim does concede that there are a few caveats. He contends that it takes a fair amount of confidence on the part of teachers to let students take the risks inherent in personalizing their own learning. Moreover, he believes that teachers have to have confidence in their students' capacity and readiness to do so and convey that confidence to them. It is that preparedness and confidence in the capacity of students to personalize their own learning that helps to make David N.'s and Jim's class experiences so successful, for both the teachers and the learners.

Perhaps the best illustration of ICE at work is the direct application of the model to actual pieces of completed work. This next section provides examples from a spectrum of subject areas and grade levels, but represent only a small sample of the applicability of the model.

\* \* \*

## Language Arts

**Figure 3.1.** The results of this grade-two spelling test are exemplary and there is no doubt that this student has successfully mastered the set of list words. Because this spelling test was restricted to assessing rote learning, the perfect score is not indicative of anything more than **I**deas-level learning.

**Figure 3.2.** This example of a grade-three student's creative writing is indicative of the initial stages of **I**deas-level demonstrations. There is an attempt to create a coherent storyline, though the writer has not made the **C**onnection between what she intends to convey and what is actually conveyed through writing; that is, the audience/reader has not been adequately considered. The structural, grammatical, and spelling errors, as well as irregular use of capital letters, indicate inconsistent use of basic writing conventions for this grade level.

> ## Some Magic Tricks Really Work
>
> One day I was at my friends labratory He was talking to me about his new Magic Trick. He said I going to do it on Cathy. The next day at school he did it and it really worked

**Figure 3.3.** The grade-five assignment that sparked this work was an invitation to write a poem about a midnight visitor. This submission went beyond the standard application of an ABAB rhyming scheme. The teacher was impressed by the variations in sentence structure, verse, and imagery to create mood and tension. It is a clear example of **E**xtensions-level work.

### THE MONSTER VISITOR

There was a rapping and a tapping
On my bedroom door.
When I opened it up,
I saw nothing more
Than a shadow cast upon the wall
By my baby sister's little toy doll.

I went back to bed,
Lay down my head,
And went back to sleep,
And didn't hear a peep.

Twelve o'clock was the time,
When from under the bed came the purple slime.
Then from under the bed came a tentacle green.
That is when I saw the monster's fangs' yellow shee
His eyes were bright red,
This was the night that I have always dread....
The night of the monster from under the bed!

My blood, he will drain,
Then he will eat my brain.
I will be devoured,
And my grave will be flowered by

Violets of blue and roses of red.
This is the future that I dread.
But, I have one weapon that will win this fight,
So, I'll reach out fast, and turn on the light!

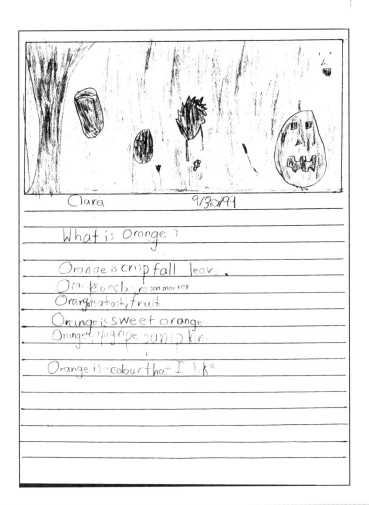

Within the illustration (handwritten by Clara):

Clara                    9/30/99

What is Orange?

Orange is crisp fall leav.
Orange beche room marker
Orange is a tasty fruit
Orange is sweet orange
Orange is a ripe pumpkin.

Orange is a colour that I like

**Figure 3.4.** This illustrated piece was produced when the students in a grade-one class had been asked to define the color orange. Clara's work clearly indicates that she's made the **C**onnections between the color orange and her own experience with orange in the world around her. She's personalized the task, thereby demonstrating its meaning to her as a learner.

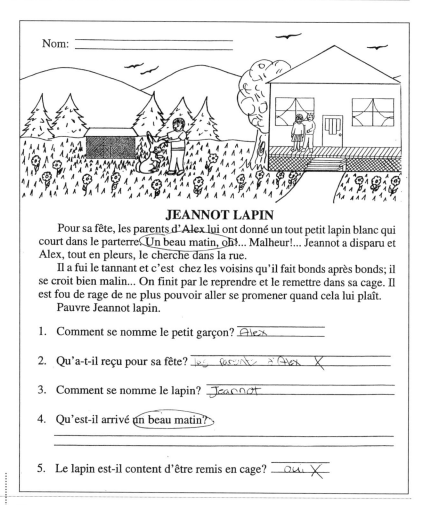

Nom: _____

**JEANNOT LAPIN**

Pour sa fête, les parents d'Alex lui ont donné un tout petit lapin blanc qui court dans le parterre. Un beau matin, oh!... Malheur!... Jeannot a disparu et Alex, tout en pleurs, le cherche dans la rue.

Il a fui le tannant et c'est chez les voisins qu'il fait bonds après bonds; il se croit bien malin... On finit par le reprendre et le remettre dans sa cage. Il est fou de rage de ne plus pouvoir aller se promener quand cela lui plaît.

Pauvre Jeannot lapin.

1. Comment se nomme le petit garçon? _Alex_

2. Qu'a-t-il reçu pour sa fête? _les parents à Alex_ X

3. Comment se nomme le lapin? _Jeannot_

4. Qu'est-il arrivé un beau matin? _____

_____

5. Le lapin est-il content d'être remis en cage? _oui_ X

**Figure 3.5.** Notice that this student was able to answer both questions that required Ideas-level responses: those asking the names of the characters in the story. However, he was not able to make the Connections to respond to questions requiring the relationship to be made between *donné* (given) and *reçu* (received), nor the other questions requiring inferences (rather than direct translation).

B.

*Dans quinze ans, j'aurai trent ans. J'habiterai en Vancouver, Columbie Britannique. Je serai un policier avec le «RCMP». J'a~~sera~~ aurai étudié à la Université de Columbie Britannique. J'~~sera~~ aurai voyagé avec John, Mary, et Collette. Nous aurons voyagé en Alberta, Columbie Brittannique, le côte-ouest des États Unis. Nous aurons habité en Califonie, et nous serons devenus un group rock s'apelle WHIP. (Warner, Harlem, Isaac, et Percy), ~~comme~~ comme Crosby, Stills, Nash, and Young, mais pas tout comme ça. Nous aurons voyagé le route à Chicago. Nous serons devenus pauvres mais après dix mois de travaillé fort, nous aurons été o.k. Nous aurons voyagé au Europe. J'aurai travaille comme serveur de boissons dans le pays d'Irelande. J'aurai gagné la lotto, et je serai devenu très riche. Mais je j'aurai été très gentil et très sympa, si je ~~je~~ je donné tout l'argent des enfants et adolescents pauvres. Et j'aurai ~~~~ parler beaucoup de français. J'aimerai ça.*

**Figure 3.6.** While there are minor **I**deas-level spelling and grammatical errors in this sample, this high-school student has been able to effectively convey meaning through the use of French. The colloquial errors indicate that he has been successful in making personal sense of the language to the extent that he can use it to convey meaning efficiently (**C**onnections), but he has not developed the idiomatic facility indicative of **E**xtensions.

**Figure 3.7.** The results from this grade-six unit test in French-as-a-second-language quite clearly demonstrate learning at the **I**deas level. Notice that in each case the student was able to identify simple verbs (**I**deas), but was unable to recognize adjuncts. It will be an easy matter for his teacher to identify the response pattern and address the obvious learning needs. The grade alone on this portion of the test would yield no such benefit.

**B. SOULIGNE LES VERBES:**

1. Ses soeurs vont être en retard. X
2. Est-ce que tu finis bientot? ✓
3. Nous ne vendons pas notre maison. ✓
4. Elle n'habite pas dans un appartement. ✓
5. Vont-ils passer leurs vacances à Toronto? ✓
6. Je vais faire une promenade. X
7. Nous dînons chez Collette. ✓
8. Quand est-ce qu'elle va aller? X
9. Faites-vous vos devoirs? ✓
10. Comment vont-elles à Montreal? ✓

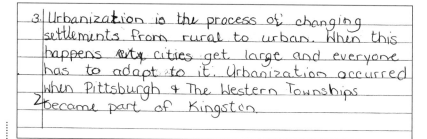

3. Urbanization is the process of changing settlements from rural to urban. When this happens city cities get large and everyone has to adapt to it. Urbanization occurred when Pittsburgh + The Western Townships became part of Kingston.

**Figure 3.8.** This response was taken from a grade-nine geography final exam. It was part of a section that asked students to provide definitions for each item in the list. This example is of particular interest: the response might be indicative of one of two levels of learning depending on how the material was covered in class. If the term *urbanization* was discussed in class with examples provided, then the answer is indicative of **I**deas-level learning; a simple reiteration of presented material. If, however, the student thought of the example on her own, it is indicative of attempts at sense-making—the result of personalizing the material by relating it to what is already known and is, therefore, demonstrative of **C**onnections-level learning.

**Figure 3.9.** Again, these examples are indicative of success at mastering **I**deas-level material. Each answer is a definition or explanation of terms studied in a grade 11 American history class and supplied by either the teacher or the textbook. Note that the invitation to define is a specific invitation to demonstrate **I**deas-level learning. There are no expectations, nor demands that the students demonstrate more.

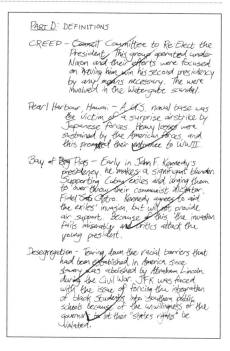

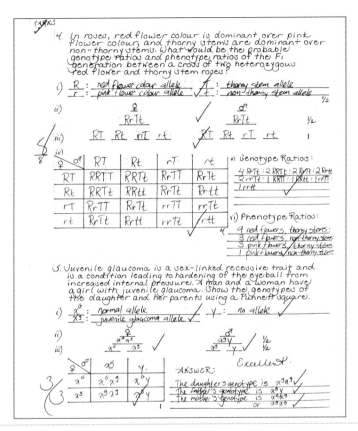

**Figure 3.10.** For those who argue that biology is a science of nothing but facts (**I**deas), this example, taken from a grade 11 biology unit test, demonstrates otherwise. The questions posed in this test require students to go beyond defining the basic concepts. They are asked to demonstrate relationships among the concepts (**C**onnections) and to the problem-question.

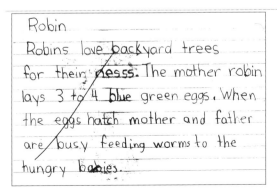

Robin

Robins love backyard trees for their nesss. The mother robin lays 3 to 4 blue green eggs. When the eggs hatch mother and father are busy feeding worms to the hungry babies.

**Figure 3.11.** This work, from a first-grade project, was the result of an assignment asking students to learn about their favorite birds. Fact lists were provided to each student before they were asked to write their brief descriptions. The exercise was ideal for eliciting **I**deas-level products.

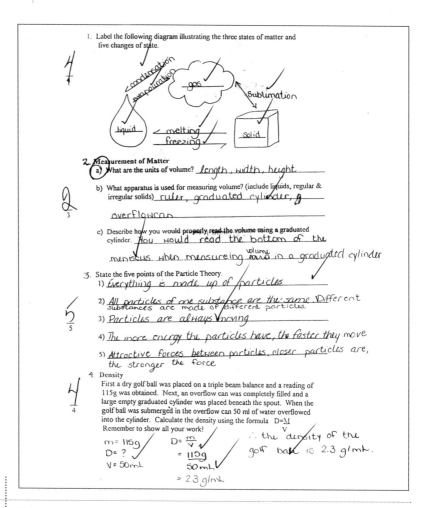

1. Label the following diagram illustrating the three states of matter and five changes of state.

condensation
evaporation
gas
Sublimation
liquid
melting
freezing
solid

2. Measurement of Matter
   a) What are the units of volume? _length, width, height_

   b) What apparatus is used for measuring volume? (include liquids, regular & irregular solids) _ruler, graduated cylinder, g_
   _overflowcan_

   c) Describe how you would properly read the volume using a graduated cylinder. _You would read the bottom of the meniscus when measureing volume in a graduated cylinder_

3. State the five points of the Particle Theory.
   1) _Everything is made up of particles_
   2) _All particles of one substance are the same. Different substances are made of different particles._
   3) _Particles are always moving_
   4) _The more energy the particles have, the faster they move_
   5) _Attractive forces between particles, closer particles are, the stronger the force_

4. Density
   First a dry golf ball was placed on a triple beam balance and a reading of 115g was obtained. Next, an overflow can was completely filled and a large empty graduated cylinder was placed beneath the spout. When the golf ball was submerged in the overflow can 50 ml of water overflowed into the cylinder. Calculate the density using the formula $D=\frac{M}{V}$
   Remember to show all your work!

   $m = 115g$
   $D = ?$
   $V = 50mL$

   $D = \frac{m}{V}$
   $= \frac{115g}{50mL}$
   $= 2.3 \ g/mL$

   ∴ the density of the golf ball is 2.3 g/mL.

**Figure 3.12.** This excerpt from a grade-nine science test clearly demonstrates the use of unambiguous questions to evoke Ideas-level responses. Even the last question, which may initially appear to invite Connections, is posed in such a way as to limit responses to demonstrations of simple calculation.

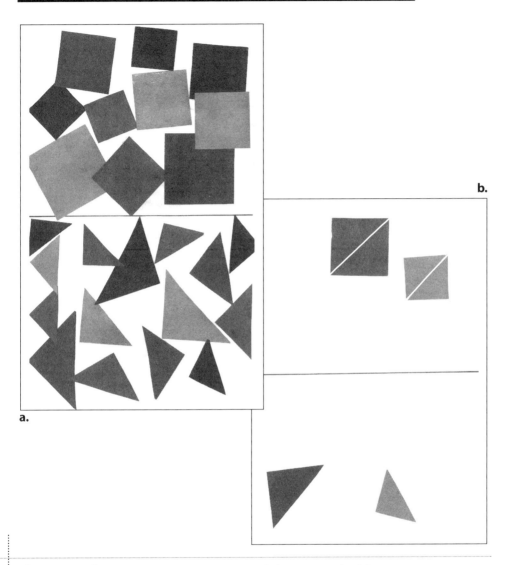

**Figure 3.13a-b.** These pieces of kindergarten work demonstrate that it is erroneous to assume that all learning at the pre-school- and primary-level must be restricted to Ideas. The task was designed so that the children might demonstrate their ability to identify and sort shapes, more specifically, squares and triangles. It was clear to the teacher that both students could differentiate between squares and triangles (Ideas), but that (b) one child also had an understanding of the relationship (Connections) between the two shapes.

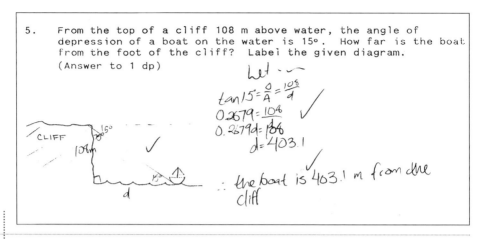

5.  From the top of a cliff 108 m above water, the angle of depression of a boat on the water is 15°. How far is the boat from the foot of the cliff? Label the given diagram. (Answer to 1 dp)

Let ...

$$\tan 15 = \frac{o}{A} = \frac{108}{d}$$

$0.2679 = \frac{108}{d}$ ✓

$0.2679 d = 108$

$d = 403.1$ ✓

CLIFF

∴ the boat is 403.1 m from the cliff

**Figure 3.14.** The high level of detail in this question, coupled with the schematic provided as part of the question, means that students' answers will be limited to demonstrations of straight application of a formula (**I**deas). To provide an opportunity for a broader range of responses, the question may be reworded to become an invitation to postulate how one might determine a boat's distance from the foot of a cliff, rather than ask for a numerical solution. This alternative of a hypothetical scenario would afford for demonstrations of **C**onnections-level learning.

It is also interesting to note that the student who provided this answer omitted the initial (**I**deas level) step of writing —"Let x be..."— and yet clearly demonstrated understanding of the material. Is it a demonstration of incomplete **I**deas-level learning or of condensing steps in the process by someone with a clear grasp of the material? Given the response patterns, we suspect the latter.

3) Using your knowledge of musical notation, complete the following bars:

**a.**

3) Using your knowledge of musical notation, complete the following bars:

**b.**

3) Using your knowledge of musical notation, complete the following bars:

**c.**

**Figure 3.15a–c.** Each of the responses to the directions for this question on the music test are correct and the teacher has awarded full marks to each student. Notice the differences among the correct responses. In the first case, the student has used a variety of notes in a demonstration that shows she understands the fundamentals of musical notation (a). While the second example may look comparable, there is also evidence that the student has taken care to devise a melody in the work, personalizing it (b). The third example, also a demonstration of Connections-level learning, illustrates that the student has been able to combine rests and notes, a clear understanding of the relationship of the two forms (c).

# Conclusion

The ICE model evolved, like most other assessment models, from teachers' beliefs about the nature of learning and how best to facilitate it through meaningful assessment. It arose as a result of teachers' realization that tests of "how much" were not serving their needs and their students' needs of "how well," and that students who knew a lot of facts were not always the ones who had accomplished the best learning.

Based on developmental theories of learning, ICE provides teachers and learners with a framework within which to understand the process of learning from a perspective other than behavioral. The result is that learning is viewed as something more than quantifiable. Viewed as a qualitative rather than quantitative process, learning can be described in terms that, in addition to outlining the criteria for assessment, also guide the learning process.

Learning is complex. Like most other complex processes, it can be broken down into elemental components, and ICE provides a framework to do exactly that. The very simplicity of the model, with three developmental stages represented by a catchy acronym, enhances its utility. The simplicity of the model is what makes it likely that teachers and students will be able to readily call it to mind and apply it to their own and others' work.

| Elements | Ideas | Connections | Extensions |
| --- | --- | --- | --- |
| | | | |
| | | | |
| | | | |

| Element | Ideas | Connections | Extensions |
|---------|-------|-------------|------------|
|         |       |             |            |
|         |       |             |            |
|         |       |             |            |
|         |       |             |            |

# Bibliography

Anderman, E. M., and M. L. Maehr. "Motivation and Schooling in the
   Middle Grades." *Review of Educational Research* 64, no. 2 (1994):
   287–307.

> This review summarizes current research into the organization of
> schools, including how organization affects assessment, and the impact
> these conditions have on pre-adolescents particularly. The case is made
> that our organizational structures tend to work against the motivations
> that sustain young people.

Benner, P. E. *From Novice to Expert: Excellence and Power in Clinical
   Nursing Practice.* Menlo Park, CA: Addison/Wesley, 1984.

> A classic book on assessing growth through the eyes of someone who
> works with nurses-in-training.

Biggs, J. B., and K. Collis. *Evaluating the Quality of Learning: SOLO
Taxonomy.* New York: Academic Press, 1982.

> The first book to link modern learning theory with classroom
> assessment practices. Its examples are drawn from real children doing
> real learning and documents how children develop in understanding of
> concepts.

Philipp, R. A., A. Flores, J. T. Sowder, and B. P. Schappelle.
"Conceptions and Practices of Extraordinary Mathematics
Teachers." *Journal of Mathematical Behavior* 13 (1994): 155–180.

> A report on how creative teachers incorporate good assessment
> practices into their teaching.

Qin, Z., D. W. Johnson, and R. T. Johnson. "Cooperative Versus Competitive Efforts and Problem Solving." *Review of Educational Research* 65, no. 2 (1995): 129–143.

> This review shows that teaching students to collaborate on learning enhances the depth with which that learning will occur.

Saurino, D. R., and P. L. Saurino. "Collaborative Teacher Research: An Investigation of Alternative Assessment." Paper presented at the annual meeting of the National Middle School Association, Cincinnati, OH, 1994.

> This report contrasts how different teachers view assessment and its effectiveness, with how researchers view the same processes.

Stiggins, R. J., and N. J. Bridgeford. "The Ecology of Classroom Assessment." *Journal of Educational Measurement* 22 (1985): 271–286.

> One of the first reports in the literature on how the classroom environment affects good assessment practices.

Tobias, S. "Interest, Prior Knowledge, and Learning." *Review of Educational Research* 64, no. 1 (1994): 37–53.

> The role of interest and prior knowledge is profound, and assessment that concentrates on growth capitalizes on these two important variables to enhance learning in classrooms.